SAFE PLACES TO LEARN

*21 Lessons to Help Students
Promote a Caring School Climate*

PAUL SULLEY

SEARCH
INSTITUTE
PRESS

Safe Places to Learn: 21 Lessons to Help Students Promote a Caring School Climate

The following are registered trademarks of Search Institute: Search Institute® and Developmental Assets®.

Paul Sulley

Search Institute Press, Minneapolis, MN
Copyright © 2007 by Search Institute

10 9 8 7 6 5 4 3 2 1
Printed on acid-free paper in the United States of America.

Search Institute
615 First Avenue Northeast, Suite 125
Minneapolis, MN 55413
www.search-institute.org
612-376-8955 • 877-240-7251

ISBN-13: 978-1-57482-157-4
ISBN-10: 1-57482-157-1

Credits
Editor: Claudia Hoffacker
Book Design: Kristine Mudd
Production Coordinator: Mary Ellen Buscher

Library of Congress Cataloging-in-Publication Data
Sulley, Paul.
  Safe places to learn : 21 lessons to help students promote a caring school climate / Paul Sulley.
    p. cm.
  ISBN-13: 978-1-57482-157-4 (pbk. : alk. paper)
  ISBN-10: 1-57482-157-1 (pbk. : alk. paper)
  1. Schools--United States--Safety measures. 2. School violence--United States--Prevention. 3. Bullying in schools--United States--Prevention. I. Title.

LB2864.5.S894 2007
363.11'9371--dc22
                          2007016660

About Search Institute Press

Search Institute Press is a division of Search Institute, a nonprofit organization that offers leadership, knowledge, and resources to promote positive youth development. Our mission at Search Institute Press is to provide practical and hope-filled resources to help create a world in which all young people thrive. Our products are embedded in research, and the 40 Developmental Assets®—qualities, experiences, and relationships youth need to succeed—are a central focus of our resources. Our logo, the SIP flower, is a symbol of the thriving and healthy growth young people experience when they have an abundance of assets in their lives.

Licensing and Copyright

Printing Tips

To produce high-quality copies of activity sheets for distribution without spending a lot of money, follow these tips:
• Always copy from the original. Copying from a copy lowers the reproduction quality.
• Make copies more appealing by using brightly colored paper or even colored ink. Quick-print shops often run daily specials on certain colors of ink.
• For variety, consider printing each activity sheet on a different color of paper.
• If you are using more than one activity sheet or an activity sheet that runs more than one page, make two-sided copies.
• Make sure the paper weight is heavy enough (use at least 60-pound offset paper) so that the words don't bleed through (as often happens with 20-pound paper).

CONTENTS

HANDOUTS, DISPLAY CHARTS, AND ACTIVITY SHEETS

These types of experiences happen to young people at school every day

On the first day at his new high school, Lee was befriended by a group of guys and girls who all seemed very nice. He was even invited to a party happening on the upcoming Saturday night. He felt good that he was accepted so quickly. When Lee arrived at the party, though, his new friends were drinking beer, and a boy handed him a bottle. He said "No thanks" and explained that he didn't drink, but the others kept challenging him to "just try it." He soon realized they weren't going to give up, so he left. On Monday, no one in the group would talk to him—or even look at him. He was completely shunned by the group just for standing up for what he believed. He became so lonely, he considered starting to drink just to fit in.

Each day when Sonya boarded the full school bus, she walked down the aisle to the teasing and taunting of other students. From a poor family, she often wore dirty clothes, and other kids would make the most hurtful, hostile comments about her appearance, her family—everything. One day, Kevin, a high school senior, continued taunting her with extremely vulgar language throughout the 45-minute bus ride. She sat quietly, ignoring him. Finally, not getting the reaction he wanted from her, he spit a giant wad of mucus into the back of her hair.

Lisa, a middle school student, was planning a small party for her closest friends. In an e-mail invitation, she asked her friends not to mention the party to Julie. "I'm really getting sick of Julie. She's not that cool anymore, so I don't want to have her at this party," Lisa wrote. However, word about the party did get back to Julie, who considered Lisa to be her best friend. Julie, of course, was devastated and angry to be excluded. The next day, she took her dad's hunting knife to school and confronted Lisa. She ended up stabbing Lisa in the arm, and Lisa was rushed to the emergency room.

INTRODUCTION

In 2004 American students ages 12–18 were victims of about 1.4 million nonfatal crimes at school.[1] This includes about 863,000 thefts and 583,000 violent crimes—107,000 of which were serious violent crimes (rape, sexual assault, robbery, and aggravated assault). In 2005 about 28 percent of students reported having been bullied at school during the past six months. (See Figure 1 on page 6.) Of the students in 2005 who reported being bullied during the previous six months, 53 percent said that they had been bullied once or twice during that period, 25 percent had experienced bullying once or twice a month, 11 percent reported being bullied once or twice a week, and 8 percent said that they had been bullied almost daily.

Of course, this is not just an American issue—it's an international one. Unfortunately, students in most countries experience violence and bullying in their schools.

School should be a place where young people feel safe; that is the only way students can be truly successful. Instead, though, many young people fear or dread going to school each day because they don't feel safe, secure, or supported. *Safe Places to Learn* offers an effective tool for creating a caring school climate—a place where students, teachers, and staff feel safe. Designed for students in grades 6–12 (ages 12–18), the lessons in this book are infused with

FIGURE 1: TYPES OF BULLYING

Of students who reported they had been bullied, here are some of the tactics they experienced:

PUSHED, SHOVED, OR SPIT ON	9%
SUBJECT OF RUMORS	15%
MADE FUN OF	19%

Source: *Indicators of School Crime and Safety: 2006* (2006). U. S. Department of Education, U.S. Department of Justice.

the Developmental Assets®—40 relationships, qualities, and attitudes all young people need to become caring, responsible, and healthy adults. (See the list of Developmental Assets on page 94.) Search Institute research shows that when a school is committed to building these assets and offering a supportive and caring environment, young people are more likely to experience better grades, improved attendance, and more positive peer relationships.

The Mission of *Safe Places to Learn*

Safe Places to Learn offers a strategy designed specifically to empower participating students to improve their school climate. The active and enthusiastic participation of students is crucial. The mission of *Safe Places to Learn* is to:

• Promote a supportive school climate;

• Build caring relationships among everyone in the school; and

• Teach all participants to build Developmental Assets in themselves and their peers.

The participants will examine the school's *norms*. The adult facilitators then ask the student participants to become *agents of change*. *Safe Places to Learn* lessons challenge students to change the norms that promote and perpetuate meanness in the school. They learn to promote positive norms such as kindness, respect, and caring while simultaneously discouraging negative norms such as gossiping, teasing, bullying, and exclusion. The lessons are designed to show the participants the power each one has to make a difference. In the end, when participants adopt and promote the positive norms, they often experience a kind of *personal transformation*, which helps them to continue the work long after the lessons and meetings are over.

Over the course of the *Safe Places* meetings, the concept of the 40 Developmental Assets is introduced, instilled, and reinforced in the minds of young people. All of the activities promote certain assets, either explicitly or implicitly.

The Importance of Developmental Assets

It's important that you as an educator encourage students' high academic achievement, but that takes more than just giving classroom lectures, administering tests, and giving assignments. To help students succeed, you must also provide a caring, supportive environment and help students get along with their peers, teachers, and others in school. Search Institute researchers have found that schools that nurture positive relationships among students—and among students and teachers—are more likely to have engaged, academically successful students.[2]

Indeed, building students' Developmental Assets contributes to their academic achievement. Research shows that young people need both a caring *and* challenging school environment for success. For example, in a national 2003 Search Institute survey, young people who said they had "caring and fair staff" at their school were more likely to also feel confident about their ability to succeed academically—73 percent had academic confidence—than were

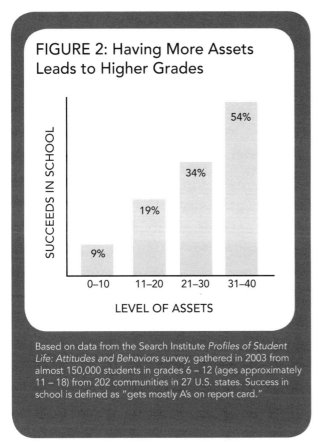

FIGURE 2: Having More Assets Leads to Higher Grades

SUCCEEDS IN SCHOOL

54%
34%
19%
9%

0–10   11–20   21–30   31–40

LEVEL OF ASSETS

Based on data from the Search Institute *Profiles of Student Life: Attitudes and Behaviors* survey, gathered in 2003 from almost 150,000 students in grades 6 – 12 (ages approximately 11 – 18) from 202 communities in 27 U.S. states. Success in school is defined as "gets mostly A's on report card."

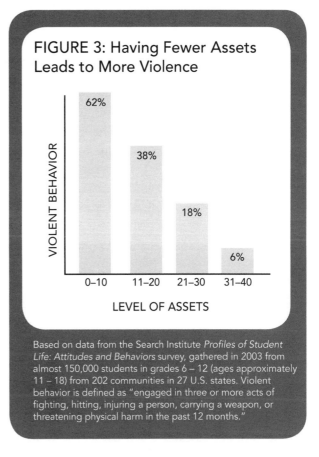

FIGURE 3: Having Fewer Assets Leads to More Violence

VIOLENT BEHAVIOR

62%
38%
18%
6%

0–10   11–20   21–30   31–40

LEVEL OF ASSETS

Based on data from the Search Institute *Profiles of Student Life: Attitudes and Behaviors* survey, gathered in 2003 from almost 150,000 students in grades 6 – 12 (ages approximately 11 – 18) from 202 communities in 27 U.S. states. Violent behavior is defined as "engaged in three or more acts of fighting, hitting, injuring a person, carrying a weapon, or threatening physical harm in the past 12 months."

students who didn't see their staff as caring and fair, only 47 percent of whom had academic confidence.[3] Figure 2 shows that the more assets young people have, the more successful they are in school.

Building Developmental Assets also gives young people the tools they need to relate well with others and to resolve conflicts peacefully, rather than turning to violence. As you can see in Figure 3, the more assets young people have, the less likely they are to engage in violent behavior.

Before You Start: Get Administrators' Buy-In

Administrative support is critical to the success of the group's efforts to improve school climate. If the principal, vice principal, or other high-level administrator welcomes students at their first meeting and speaks to them about the importance of their involvement, that will empower them as they embark on their mission. Ideally, the administrator will periodically attend and participate in future meetings as well.

Student Selection

You may engage in the *Safe Places to Learn* lessons with an existing student group—such as student council or peer helpers—or you can form a group with the specific mission of improving school climate. If you are forming a new group, ideally you will identify students who are opinion leaders in their groups. In other words, the participants have some influence over their own circle of friends. The benefit of identifying student opinion leaders is that they tend to be trendsetters who establish norms in the school. If those leaders are challenged and inspired to be a positive force, their influence is likely to ripple throughout the school.

Methods to identify student opinion leaders include the following:

1 **Create a committee of adults and conduct a survey.** Use of a survey is the best way to identify a cross section of students whose opinions are valued by others. The adults on the committee should know the students well and have insight into the dynamics of their relationships. Keep in mind that the survey is a subjective tool, and it can be flexible. Don't feel that you have to go by absolute numbers. Those who review the survey results can identify student leaders from different groups even though their names may not have appeared as often as others. The disadvantages of using the survey are that it can be logistically challenging and time consuming. (See the survey and instructions for administering it starting on page 89.)

2 **Create a committee of adults and students.** This method includes valuable student opinion. The committee can use the survey questions to launch a discussion to identify both students and staff.

3 **Create a committee of adults.** For this method, also, the adults need to know the students well and have insight into the dynamics of their relationships.

4 **Have one adult select the students.** Again, it is crucial that this adult know the students well and have insight into the dynamics of their relationships. This method may work well for small schools.

How to Use This Book

Teachers, counselors, or other school adults can lead the *Safe Places to Learn* initiative. The 21 lessons are grouped according to the general headings of *Introductory Lessons, Reflections, Team Building, School Engagement,* and *Closure.* The first two lessons provide a solid introduction to the mission, while Lesson 3 gets participants into the right frame of mind and sets the tone for the remaining lessons. Therefore, it is important that the first three lessons be presented in that order. After that, you do not have to present lessons in the order they appear here. You may select lessons based on your group's priorities. Notice, however, that certain lessons are a prerequisite for other lessons.

The *Reflections* section includes four lessons that examine norms, assets, and the commitment of each participant. The three *Team Building* lessons will help participants get to know each other better and build cohesiveness in the group. The *School Engagement* section includes 11 lessons that help students *do something good* in and for their school. The final section, *Closure,* provides an activity that is intended to be presented during the last formal meeting of the group.

An adult or team of adults should facilitate Lessons 1, 2, 3, and 12. Students may facilitate any of the other activities. It is probably best to have two or more students work together as co-facilitators. They will need some time to prepare and may need some guidance from an adult. Having students facilitate is a great way to empower all of the student participants to truly take ownership of the mission.

Make sure to read through each lesson before presenting it. (See "Tips for Group Leaders" on page 10.) In each lesson, you will see (in italics) suggested language for the facilitator to say to the group. Possible answers to questions are in bold. You know your group, so be creative and feel free to modify the lessons as you see fit. Make sure, however, that modifications don't deviate from the objective stated at the beginning of each lesson. Also remember that part of the activity is discussing how the activity applies to the *mission* of creating a more supportive and caring school climate. Don't skip this important part of the lesson.

After several meetings, you may find it helpful to review lessons and activity sheets from previous meetings to reinforce the lessons students have learned. You can repeat Lesson 2, Review and Renew, several times, as this lesson can take as little as 15 minutes when presented in a small team meeting. If you collect all activity sheets in personal folders, you can return folders to students at the end of the year for further reflection.

Handling Absences and Late Joiners

Through the course of the lessons, it's important to empower students to be accountable for their own participation. Encourage students to team up in pairs so that if one must miss a meeting, her or his teammate will share the missed information.

If a student stops coming to meetings altogether, encourage other students from the group to invite that student to return. It is a good idea for you as the adult advisor to meet with the student to determine why the student stopped coming. Help the student weigh the advantages and disadvantages of staying with or leaving the group. Ultimately, if the student isn't a willing participant, it is probably best to let her or him leave.

If students ask to join the group after meetings have already commenced, it is up to you whether to allow it. If you feel it will benefit the group, or at least not hinder it, there is nothing wrong with allowing newcomers. You may want to get input from the other adults and students in the group. If everyone feels that a new person would be open to working toward the mission, would strengthen the group, and be a cohesive factor, then it's probably a good idea to allow her or him to join. In all likelihood, students who express an interest in joining probably will be excited about the mission and so will be good additions. Take time to meet with new students to go over any information they missed in previous meetings.

A Word about Bullying

The lessons in *Safe Places to Learn* address the broad issue of helping to build a more supportive school climate. The emphasis is to create a climate that promotes positive norms and does not accept negative norms, including bullying. Several lessons—directly or indirectly—address bullying or tolerating a bully. These include Lessons 1, 3, 13, 14, and 17.

Ongoing Meetings and the Small Team Approach

To make an impact on your school, you would ideally have 50 or more students participating in the activities. If you don't have the space at your school to accommodate 50 or more students, you can divide your participants into small teams, each consisting of one adult and five to eight students. Consider intentionally grouping students with people they don't normally associate or socialize with to help build new relationships that will strengthen the larger group.

Each group, independently, should meet and do the appropriate activities every week or at least every other week. It is ideal if all groups can meet together on a monthly basis to discuss progress and the lessons they have learned.

Optional Materials

At the beginning of each lesson, there is a list of materials you will need for the meeting. There are two optional items that you will need to order ahead of time if you choose to use them.

1 Poster of the 40 Developmental Assets. To order a color poster from Search Institute, call 877-240-7251 or visit the online store at www.searchinstitutestore.org.

2 Wristbands that say *No act of kindness, no matter how small, is ever wasted* and those that say *Be the change you wish to see in the world*. You may order these wristbands online at www.itpaystobekind.com.

Suggestions for alternatives to these optional items are provided in the lessons.

The inspiration for *Safe Places to Learn*—the *Change of Heart* training

Safe Places to Learn was inspired by Search Institute's *Change of Heart* training. While it isn't necessary to do both the training and the *Safe Places* lessons, using the two together enhances your efforts to create a more caring climate for your school. If possible, have the training retreat and then follow up with the lessons in this book. If your school is interested in *Change of Heart* training, contact Vision Training Associates at 800-294-4322. For more information, visit www.search-institute.org/training/sessions/changeofheart.html.

TIPS FOR GROUP LEADERS

1. Be prepared. Practice. Know what you are going to say and when you are going to say it. Have handouts, charts, and other materials readily available. If students are facilitating a lesson, work with them to make sure they are prepared.

2. Create a caring environment. (Walk the talk!) Consider using uplifting background music as students enter the room or when the group is working on a task. Welcome students warmly as they arrive. Consider asking a student volunteer to act as a greeter. Reinforce the agreements to maintain a supportive and caring environment.

3. Know your students. The lessons are not cast in concrete. Adapt the lesson to make it relevant to the students' lives.

4. Set the tone for each lesson. Remind the students of the purpose of this group and the importance of the work they are doing in the school. Encourage full participation by all students and adults.

5. Make it real. Tell true stories that are relevant to the day's lesson. Ask students to share their stories to reinforce the messages.

6. Allow time for students to respond. Don't worry if there are a few minutes of silence; they give students time to respond. Use open-ended discussion techniques. Restate the question if necessary.

7. Close with purpose and feeling. Close so that all are inspired, uplifted, and motivated to continue to make a difference. Consider using appropriate quotations or poems to provide inspiration. Check the news for stories about kindness or violence that may be relevant to this group.

8. Be intentional. Keep in mind that all activities are to be done on purpose and with purpose.

9. Be flexible. Fully entertain questions and pursue meaningful discussion, even if it means you have to change your plans for the day's lesson slightly.

10. Have fun! Relax, be yourself, use your sense of humor, and allow participants to have fun.

NOTES

1. *Indicators of School Crime and Safety: 2006* (2006). U.S. Department of Education, U.S. Department of Justice.

2. Scales, P. C., & Leffert, N. (2004). *Developmental assets: A synthesis of the scientific research on adolescent development* (2d ed.). Minneapolis, MN: Search Institute.

3. Search Institute. (2006). *Creating a great place to learn: Resources for moving forward.* Minneapolis, MN: Author.

INTRODUCTORY LESSONS

MISSION *IS* POSSIBLE

READY

Summary: This lesson is an introduction to the *mission* to promote a more supportive school climate, build more caring relationships, and learn the importance of the 40 Developmental Assets. Participants are challenged to become *change agents* and to promote the positive *norms* of kindness, caring, and respect.

SET

Time Required: 60 minutes

Assets Promoted: Caring School Climate, Community Values Youth, Youth as Resources, Positive Peer Influence, High Expectations, Caring, Personal Power

Materials Needed:

List or poster of the 40 Developmental Assets
Poster board and/or flip-chart paper
Handout 1: 40 Developmental Assets for Adolescents
Handout 2: Agreements
Display Chart 1: Mission
Display Chart 2: Agreements

Display Chart 3: Discussion Question #1
Display Chart 4: Quote from Aesop
Display Chart 5: Quote from Gandhi
Display Chart 6: Quote from Margaret Mead
Paper for recorders
Beach ball

Optional: Wristband that says *No act of kindness, no matter how small, is ever wasted.* (Other options for kindness gifts/reminders are a leather cord bracelet, safety pin with beads, ribbon, friendship bracelet, or some other creative token that participants can make.)

Preparation:

- Read the lesson and think about how to facilitate it to meet your group's and school's particular needs. Keep in mind that the scripted parts (shown in italics) of the lesson provide only suggested language. Feel free to modify to fit your own style and your group's unique goals.
- Before the session, ask three students to demonstrate the support fall during the meeting (see ❹).
- Be prepared to tell a story of a kind act that you've witnessed or heard about (see ❿).
- If you are going to use the 40 Developmental Assets poster, make sure you have ordered and received it (see page 9 for ordering information). Otherwise, make your own large list of the 40 assets using poster board or flip-chart paper. Display it where all participants can see it. (You will use this for all meetings.)
- Make Display Charts 1–6 (see pages 109–111), using poster board or flip-chart paper, and hang them around the room where all participants can see them. (Keep them after this meeting. You will use them again for future meetings.)
- Make copies of Handout 1 (see pages 94–95), one per participant.
- If you plan to distribute the "kindness" wristbands, make sure you have ordered and received them (see page 9 for ordering information). If you are going to make your own kindness gifts/reminders, make sure you have the materials to do that.

GO

(1) Welcome participants to the session. Introduce yourself and your co-leaders, if any.

Then **SAY** *We are here today for a reason and a purpose. It is not by accident that you are here today. All of you are seen as leaders in this school. Whether you know it or not, other students listen to you, watch what you do, and follow your lead. With leadership comes a great opportunity to influence others. Not only do you have a great opportunity, but I believe you also have an obligation and an awesome responsibility to make a difference, to do the right thing, and to promote the common good.*

(2) **TALK** to the students about the power they have to create a positive school climate: *Everyone in this room has an individual power. We call this the "power of one." Each of us, if we choose to use this power, has the potential to help, to heal, to support, to challenge, and to change—for the better—the life of another person.*

You have this power, if you choose to use it. If we multiply the power of one by the number of people in this room, we create the power of many. The power is truly here among us to change the culture of the school, for better or worse. It's our choice!

The Mission

(3) Referring to Display Chart 1, Mission, **SAY** *Why are we here? To promote a safer and more supportive school climate, to help build more caring relationships, and to understand the importance of the Developmental Assets.*

Take a moment to refer to the list of assets displayed and distribute Handout 1. **SAY** *Take a moment to look over this list when you have a chance. We will discuss this in detail during a later meeting.*

ASK *What do we mean by school* **climate***?* (**The feeling in the school**.)

The climate is the feeling in the school: Do we feel welcome? Do we feel like we belong here? Do we feel cared for? Do we feel supported? Do we even want to be here?

Unfortunately, for too many students, the answer to all of these questions is no.

We know that if we feel supported, connected, and cared for, we thrive. We all do better! We want people to be successful. That's why we are here today.

(4) Explain to the participants that three volunteers were asked to demonstrate what support looks like in simple terms. Ask the three volunteers to come forward.

Align volunteers in the front of the room so all can see. Explain that one person will fall into the hands of the two supporters. Say that the volunteer faller will depend upon the supporters for her or his physical safety. Explain the calls of the faller and the two supporters. Ask the faller to stand upright and rigid with arms folded across her or his chest. Ask that the supporters stand behind the faller ready to support that person.

Explain the calls (without the volunteers actually moving) as follows:

Faller: My name is (say first name) and I am ready for a challenge!
Supporters: We're here for you, (faller's name)!
Faller: Are you ready to support me?
Supporters: Yes!
Faller: Falling!
Supporters: Fall away!

Once you have explained the calls and all the volunteers understand what they are supposed to do, then have the volunteers do their calls with the faller actually falling back and the supporters catching her or him. The faller needs only to fall about 10 inches to demonstrate the result. Stand by the faller and coach the volunteers through the calls. Be close to ensure the safety of the faller and the supporters.

After the demonstration, thank the volunteers and ask for applause for their efforts. **EXPLAIN** *This is what support looks like in simple terms.*

(5) Point to the word *Norms* on Display Chart 1 and **ASK** *What is a "norm"?* (**A generally accepted standard of behavior.**) Give an example of a norm (such as, driving on the right side of the road or shaking hands when you meet someone).

ASK a series of questions about the uncaring norms you know of in your school. For example:

In this school, is it the norm to gossip about someone?
In this school, is it the norm to tease someone in a hurtful way?
In this school, is it the norm to ignore or exclude others?
In this school, is it the norm to push, trip, pinch, slap, kick, or punch someone?

EXPLAIN the goal of changing these norms: *A large part of our mission is to act as* **change agents** (point to the words *Change Agents* on Display Chart 1), *to* **change the norms** *that promote and perpetuate meanness. Your role as a* **change agent** *is to promote more positive norms, like respect, kindness, common courtesy, and caring. In addition to promoting positive norms, your role is to discourage negative norms, some of which we just reviewed.*

Agreements

6 Next, it is important to have the students agree that they will help create a positive climate in these group meetings. As you distribute Handout 2, Agreements, **SAY** *In a few minutes we are going to get into small groups to discuss a topic. First, though, we need to come to some agreements that will help us all to:*

• *Be comfortable;*
• *Be ourselves;*
• *Feel safe, supported, and respected.*

Refer to Display Chart 2, Agreements, and **SAY** *The first agreement is safety. We all want and need to be safe.*

ASK the following:

Besides physically, how else can you hurt someone? **(You can hurt someone emotionally, or, as we commonly say, you can hurt someone's feelings.)**
How can you hurt someone's feelings here today? **(By teasing or criticizing her or him.)**
How else can you hurt someone's feelings here today? **(By ignoring her or him.)**
How else can you hurt someone's feelings here today? **(By gossiping about her or him.)**
How else can you hurt someone's feelings here today? **(By excluding her or him.)**

SAY *We need to be safe here. Can we agree not to hurt anyone, either physically or emotionally?*

Continue to the next word on Display Chart 2:

The second agreement is support. We all need to feel supported. How can we support people here? **(Offering verbal encouragement; listening to others.)**

SAY *We all need to feel supported. Can we agree to support people here today?*

Next, discuss the third word on Display Chart 2: *The last agreement is respect. How can we show respect to people here?* **(Listening to people; allowing one person to talk at a time; maintaining confidentiality so what is said here stays here.)**

SAY *We need to be respectful of each other. Can we agree to show respect to everyone here?*

Now can we commit to these agreements? Show me a thumbs-up if you are committed to following these agreements. Thank you!

Small Group Activity

7 **INTRODUCE** the group activity with the following: *I know the people here are doing good and honorable deeds to promote the positive norms that we talked about. I also know that there is always room for improvement. I would be the first to admit that there is room for improvement for me to be more respectful, helpful, kind, and considerate toward others in this school.*

Referring to Display Chart 3, Discussion Question #1, **SAY** *At this point, let's talk about what we are doing right. I'd like you to form into groups of four and answer this question: What are you doing in your school to promote the positive norms of kindness, respect, common courtesy, caring, and support?*

Have participants form groups of four. If other adults are participants, request that one adult join each group as the fourth member. Explain that two people per group are needed to volunteer: one as a recorder, the other as a reporter. The recorder writes the information given by the members of the small group. When they are done, the reporter shares that information with the entire group.

8 Allow 8 to 10 minutes for participants to share. Circulate around the room to make sure all groups are on task. When time is up or when groups have finished their discussion, ask each reporter to share her or his group's findings.

(Optional: You may record the information on chart paper.) After each reporter is done, if a caring act is particularly interesting, ask the participant who offered that act to tell her or his story. Afterward, thank the participant for what he or she has done and ask for applause from the group.

9 **ASK** *What's the point of doing this activity and what does it have to do with our mission of creating a more caring and supportive school climate?* **(To demonstrate that we are already helping to create a caring school; there is a lot more each of us can do; we need to be aware of the power we have to make a difference; every act of kindness counts; if we all work together we can have a greater impact; we need to discourage the negative stuff; it feels good to be caring and kind.)**

10 Tell a story that illustrates the power of a kind act.

Refer to the quote on Display Chart 4: "No act of kindness, no matter how small, is ever wasted." (Aesop)

ASK *Can we waste kindness? Can we be too kind?*

After a slight pause to let the group think about these questions, continue: *Have you heard the saying "What goes around comes around"? What does that mean?* **(If you are kind to others, that kindness spreads around and, eventually, comes back to you; if you are mean to people, that, too, can spread.)**

SAY *Part of our mission is to be kind and to spread kindness around the school. Our challenge to you is for you, every day, to offer three simple acts of kindness to others in the school. We're not asking you to jump in front of a moving vehicle to save someone's life, but just to make some simple efforts to brighten another person's day, such as:*
• *Offer a smile;*
• *Say a kind word;*
• *Talk to someone who seems to be lonely; or*
• *Stick up for someone who is being teased or picked on.*

SAY *Do you think if everyone did three acts of kindness every day it would have an impact on the school? If I multiply three times the number of people in this room that number is _____!*

Would (number) acts of kindness make a difference in this school? Multiply this number by five days a week, four weeks a month, and nine months a school year. That's a lot of kindness!

Beach Ball Activity

11 Tell students that for the next activity everyone will sit on the floor. (Allow the option for adults or others with physical limitations to sit in chairs and still participate.) **SAY** *We need to sit together and fill up the floor space so that there are no large gaps between people. For safety purposes, make sure you are sitting down all the way, and not up on your knees.*

ASK with beach ball in hand: *Who knows what a metaphor is?* **(A figure of speech comparing two unrelated objects or ideas.)** *Can you give me an example of a metaphor?* **("The world's a stage," "You are my sunshine.")** *This beach ball is a metaphor for kindness. Your task is to tap the beach ball 50 times without its touching the ground. If it touches the ground, we will start over again.* (You may want to tap it more or less than 50 times, depending on your time and the size of the group.)

EXPLAIN the rules: *The ball represents the kind acts we will all offer. We need to pass the ball (the kindness) around our circle here, the way we will pass acts of kindness around the school. You cannot tap the ball two consecutive times, and you can't pass the ball between just two or three people. Also, we all need to count together in unison.*

Toss the beach ball into the air over the group and have everyone count the taps aloud. If the ball touches the ground, start over.

Each time the ball falls to the ground, **ASK** the group: *What do we need to do to make this work?* Do this until the group completes the task.

12 **ASK** *What did we learn from this activity and how does it apply to our mission of creating a more caring and supportive school climate?* **(If we work together we can be more successful; everyone counts; everyone can make a difference; the little acts count; all the acts add up to have a larger effect; keep your eye on the ball—the mission!)**

(13) While everyone is seated, thank the group for its participation, for sharing and caring. **ASK** *Do you think we can really make a difference in our school? Should we even try?* (Reach a general consensus of yes!)

Kindness Reminder

If you choose to give participants "kindness" wristbands or another reminder, you may present them now. You may either give them the wristbands or other reminders (see suggestions under Preparation at the beginning of this lesson) that you've made, or you may provide the materials to make a reminder. If you provide materials, have participants make them now or take them home and make them.

SAY *I have a gift for you. This gift will act as a reminder to be kind and to make a difference.*

Show the kindness reminder and read the quote from Aesop: *No act of kindness, no matter how small, is ever wasted.*

Then **SAY** *I would like to give you one, but only if you are willing to make a commitment to make a difference, to be part of our effort, our mission, and to offer at least three acts of kindness toward others every day.*

EXPLAIN further: *I would also like you to wear it each day and to acknowledge those in our group when you see them wearing their reminders. When you see each other in the halls, point to your reminder and ask, "Have you done your three acts of kindness today?"*

While everyone remains seated on the floor, pass out the reminders (or materials and, if needed, instructions to make them), one for each participant.

(14) Discuss when and where the next meeting will be. If possible, set the time and place now.

Closure

(15) While the group remains seated, **SAY** *I would like to thank everyone again for being here, for your commitment, and for caring. It has truly been an honor to be here with you.*

In closing, I would like to share two powerful quotes from two role models of kindness. While referring to Display Chart 5, read the quote from Mahatma Gandhi: *"Be the change you wish to see in the world." If we truly want to have a more peaceful and compassionate world it has to begin with each and every one of us!*

Next, while referring to Display Chart 6, read the quote from Margaret Mead: *"Never doubt that a small group of committed people can change the world; indeed, it's the only thing that ever has!" I see the people here as the small group that can make big changes!*

If there is time, **ASK** *Would anyone like to say anything—words of encouragement, thoughts, feelings—to our group in closing?* Allow several participants to share.

Thank the group for its commitment and willingness to help make the school a better place. Once again, state the date, time, and location of the next meeting.

REVIEW AND RENEW

Note: This lesson can stand alone, but it is also recommended that you repeat this lesson from time to time as an introduction for any future meeting.

READY

Summary: Participants share what they have done recently to make a difference in their school.

SET

Time Required: 30 minutes

Assets Promoted: Caring School Climate, Community Values Youth, Youth as Resources, Service to Others, Positive Peer Influence, High Expectations, Caring

Materials Needed:

List or poster of the 40 Developmental Assets
Display Chart 1: Mission

Display Chart 2: Agreements
Display Chart 7: Discussion Question #2

Preparation:

- Read the lesson and think about how to facilitate it to meet your group's and school's particular needs. Keep in mind that the scripted parts (shown in italics) of the lesson provide only suggested language. Feel free to modify to fit your own style and your group's unique goals.
- Make Display Chart 7 (see page 112), using poster board or flip-chart paper.
- Display the 40 Developmental Assets, as well as Display Charts 1, 2, and 7, where all participants can see them.

GO

Welcome and Review

1 Welcome participants and thank them for being here. **SAY** *We are here today to continue with our efforts to improve our school climate.*

ASK *What is our mission?*

Referring to Display Chart 1, Mission, **REMIND** the group that the mission is *to promote a safer and more supportive school climate, to help build more caring relationships,* and *to understand the importance of the Developmental Assets.*

ASK *What did we discuss at our last meeting?* (Review.)

Explain that the purpose of ongoing meetings is to remind ourselves of the importance of continuing to make a difference in our school. **SAY** *Today we are going to give you an opportunity to review what you have done in the school to make a difference.*

2 Have participants form into groups of four. If any adults are present, include one in each group.

Refer to Display Chart 2, Agreements, and remind participants of the agreements of safety, support, and respect that you discussed previously.

Referring to Display Chart 7, Discussion Question #2, ASK *What have you done to make a difference in your school since our last meeting?*

Be sure each group has a recorder and a reporter. Give participants about 10 minutes to discuss the question.

3 After about 8 minutes, ask each group to select one especially kind act or experience of all the things group members shared. Identify this act as "magnanimous," which is defined as "to disdain meanness and display a noble generosity; a large and generous spirit or heart." Give participants 2 or more minutes to choose this act.

4 Ask the reporters to report all the acts of kindness to the whole group. Ask each reporter to identify the magnanimous act last.

If it is appropriate, ask the participant who offered the magnanimous act, or if there are any other inspiring acts, to tell the story of what happened. Ask the participant to give the details of what happened so everyone feels the emotion that the people giving and receiving the kindness felt. Applaud each participant who shares.

5 When the group is done sharing, ASK *What is the point of doing this activity and how does it apply to our mission of helping to create a more caring and supportive school?* **(It reminds us to be proactive; inspires us to do more; demonstrates that we can and do make a difference; shows us that little things do count.)**

Thank the participants for sharing and caring.

6 Discuss when and where the next meeting will be. If possible, set the time and place now.

7 Close with the entire group standing in a circle.

SAY *If anyone would like to share anything (feelings, thoughts, words of encouragement, etc.), you may do so now.*

Thank the group for its commitment and willingness to help make the school a better place. Once again, state the date, time, and location of the next meeting.

REFLECTIONS

BE THE CHANGE

Note: Lesson 13 is a direct follow-up to this activity.

READY

Summary: Participants examine their personal norms that promote either positive or negative social interactions. Participants are then challenged to promote the positive norms and discourage the negative norms in their everyday life.

SET

Time Required: 45 minutes

Assets Promoted: Caring School Climate, Community Values Youth, Youth as Resources, Service to Others, High Expectations, Positive Peer Influence, Caring, Honesty, Responsibility, Interpersonal Competence, School Boundaries, Personal Power

Materials Needed:

List or poster of the 40 Developmental Assets
Activity Sheet 1: Guidelines for Caring (Part 1): Self-Inventory
Activity Sheet 2: Guidelines for Caring (Part 2): The Plan

Display Chart 1: Mission
Display Chart 2: Agreements
File folders, one per participant

Optional: Wristbands that say *Be the change you wish to see in the world.* (Other options for reminders to be a positive influence are a leather cord bracelet, safety pin with beads, ribbon, friendship bracelet, or some other creative token that participants can make.)

Preparation:

• Read the lesson and think about how to facilitate it to meet your group's and school's particular needs. Keep in mind that the scripted parts (shown in italics) of the lesson provide only suggested language. Feel free to modify to fit your own style and your group's unique goals.

• Make copies of Activity Sheets 1 and 2 (see pages 116–118), one each per participant.

• Display the 40 Developmental Assets, as well as Display Charts 1 and 2, where all participants can see them.

• Create a personal file folder for each participant, and choose or create a secure place to store them.

• If you plan to distribute the "Be the change" wristbands, make sure you have ordered and received them (see page 9 for ordering information). If you are going to make your own reminders, make sure you have the materials to do that.

GO

Review of Previous Meetings

1 Welcome participants, thank them for being here, and REMIND them: *We are here today to continue with our efforts to improve our school. What is our mission?*

Refer to Display Chart 1, Mission, and SAY *Our mission is to promote a safer and more supportive school climate, to help build more caring relationships, and to understand the importance of the Developmental Assets.*

ASK *What did we discuss at our last meeting?* (Review.)

Explain that the purpose of ongoing meetings is to remind ourselves of the importance of continuing to make a difference in our school.

Refer to Display Chart 2, Agreements, and give a brief review.

2 ASK *Does anyone remember the definition of a norm from our earlier discussion? What is a norm?* **(A generally accepted standard of behavior.)**

ASK *Can you give me an example of a norm?* **(Driving on the right side of the road; shaking hands when you meet someone; smiling when a photo is taken.)**

EXPLAIN *If we are truly going to make a difference in our school, we need to change the norms that promote and perpetuate mean and uncaring acts. We need to start by examining our own norms and behaviors.*

Guidelines for Caring: Self-Inventory

3 EXPLAIN *Today we will have an opportunity to check our personal norms. We will be able to examine what each of us can do to promote the positive and discourage the negative norms through this self-inventory called Guidelines for Caring.*

Pass out Activity Sheet 1, Guidelines for Caring (Part 1): Self-Inventory.

SAY *The Guidelines for Caring are divided into two parts. The first part, which you are receiving now, is a questionnaire. Part 2, which you will receive later, is a plan of what you want to do as a result of what you learn in Part 1.*

Ask for a volunteer to read the first two paragraphs of Guidelines for Caring (Part 1): Self-Inventory. Then ask someone else to read the third paragraph and the directions.

EXPLAIN *After you circle your last response, please review the statements and your responses. Then complete the statement at the bottom of the questionnaire.* Ask whether they have questions. Then give participants 6 to 8 minutes to complete the task.

4 When everyone is done with the assignment, have participants form into groups of four. If adults are present, include one in each group. Tell participants that they will share with their small group the insights they gained from doing this activity.

ASK *What did you learn from this activity?* Allow about 10 minutes for all members of the group to discuss their findings.

When time is up, ASK *Would anyone like to share with the entire group what you learned or realized from doing this activity and from your discussion?* (Take several responses.)

Guidelines for Caring: The Plan

5 SAY *Next, you will receive the second part of Guidelines for Caring. Part 2 will help us apply what we learned from Part 1.*

Pass out Activity Sheet 2, Guidelines for Caring (Part 2): The Plan. Ask for a volunteer to read the directions.

EXPLAIN *The heading "Discouraging Negativity" corresponds to the same heading for the first three statements of the Self-Inventory you did in Part 1. The heading "Promoting the Positive" corresponds to the same heading for the next set of statements of the Self-Inventory. The same is true for the heading "Being Courageous, Doing the Right Thing."*

Your task is to look over the statements under each of the three headings and write what you are willing to do to be that more positive force in school and in your relationships with others. Any questions?

When you are done, you will have an opportunity to share your plans in small groups.

6 When participants have finished, ask them to return to their small groups and share their plans.

EXPLAIN *After you share your plan, please sign it. Also, ask others in your group to sign your plan as witnesses. The witnesses' job is to help you be accountable for your plan; that is, to remind you to follow through with what you say you are going to do.*

7 When the groups are done, ask if anyone would like to share one thing from her or his plan to make a difference.

After several responses and discussion, thank the group for being honest and forthright.

8 **ASK** the group: *What did we learn from this activity and how does this relate to our mission of promoting a more caring and supportive school climate?* **(We need to be aware of how we promote our bad habits, the negative norms; we need to be intentional about promoting the positive norms; if we all follow through on our plan, we will make a difference.)**

Optional Wristband

9 If you choose to give participants "Be the change" wristbands or another reminder to be a positive influence, you may present them now. You may either give them the wristbands or other reminders (see suggestions under Preparation at the beginning of this lesson) that you've made, or you may provide the materials to make a reminder. If you provide materials, have participants make them now or take them home and make them.

ASK *Do you think we can really change our own bad habits, our indifference and negativity? Do you think we can really be a more positive force in the school? Raise your hand if you think so.*

Keep your hand raised because I have a gift for you that can act as a reminder to be that positive person

and influence in the school. (Pass out the wristbands or other reminders.)

As participants are receiving their gifts, **SAY** *This gift is to remind you to do what Gandhi said: Be the change you wish to see in the world. Our mission is to help create a more caring school. Remember, you are here for a reason and a purpose. Every day you have many opportunities to truly make a difference and to be that positive force in your world. Please wear this gift as a reminder for you to . . . be the change!*

Wear it to remind you and all of us of our purpose and our important work in the school.

10 Collect the activity sheets, Guidelines for Caring (Parts 1 and 2), and file them in participants' personal folders. **SAY** *In future meetings we will have a chance to review our handouts.*

Thank the group for sharing and for making a difference.

Discuss when and where the next meeting will be. If possible, set the time and place now.

Closure

11 Close with the entire group standing in a circle. **ASK** *Would anyone like to share anything with the group (feelings, thoughts, words of encouragement, etc.)?* (Allow a few people to speak.)

Thank the group for its commitment and willingness to help make the school a better place. Once again, state the date, time, and location of the next meeting.

GO FOR 40!

READY

Summary: Go over the list of 40 Development Assets, which you briefly introduced to participants in Lesson 1. Each participant identifies three assets that are strong in her or his life (*strength* assets). Each participant also identifies one asset he or she would like to have, and develops a plan to attain that asset.

SET

Time Required: 30 minutes

Assets Promoted: Varies, depending on the assets on which each individual chooses to focus.

Materials Needed:

List or poster of the 40 Developmental Assets
Handout 1: 40 Developmental Assets for Adolescents
Activity Sheet 3: Asset Goal

Display Chart 1: Mission
Display Chart 2: Agreements

Preparation:

- Read the lesson and think about how to facilitate it to meet your group's and school's particular needs. Keep in mind that the scripted parts (shown in italics) of the lesson provide only suggested language. Feel free to modify to fit your own style and your group's unique goals.
- Make copies of Handout 1 (see pages 94–95) and Activity Sheet 3 (see page 119), one per participant.
- Display the 40 Developmental Assets, as well as Display Charts 1 and 2, where all participants can see them.

GO

Review of Previous Meetings

1 Welcome participants, thank them for being here, and **REMIND** them: *We are here today to continue with our efforts to improve our school. What is our mission?*

Refer to Display Chart 1, Mission, and **SAY** *Our mission is to promote a safer and more supportive school climate, to help build more caring relationships, and to understand the importance of the Developmental Assets.*

ASK *What did we discuss at our last meeting?* (Review.)

Explain that the purpose of ongoing meetings is to remind ourselves of the importance of continuing to make a difference in our school.

Refer to Display Chart 2, Agreements, and give a brief review.

Introducing Developmental Assets

2 **SAY** *Today we are going to give you an opportunity to examine some of your strengths and to focus on an area of your life that you would like to strengthen. To begin our discussion, I'd like to ask* *you some questions. Raise your hand if the answer is yes. Would you like to be unhappy?...unhealthy?... poor?... doing something you don't enjoy? None of us wants that!*

Then **ASK** *How many here would like to be happy?... healthy?... financially stable?... have a job you enjoy?... have a healthy family?*

SAY *There are no guarantees in life, but if you follow some basic principles and incorporate them into your life, you'll increase the probability that you will lead a successful and happy life.*

3 Call a student by name and **ASK** *How much money would you give if you could have the secret for a successful life?* After the student responds, repeat the amount.

SAY *You would give ($) for a life of health and happiness?*

ASK *How much money would others give?* Take a few responses.

Then **SAY** *I have the secret. In fact, you will all have the secret in just a few moments. The secret is in what we call the 40 Developmental Assets.*

4 **ASK** *When I say the word "asset," does anyone know what I mean?*

Continue:
Raise your hand if you think of... money! (pause) Good!
Raise your hand if you think of... having valuable things. (pause) Good!
Raise your hand if you think of... strengths! (pause) Excellent!

Most of you know the word "assets" as having a house, or investments, or a bank account, or good qualities as in "his sense of humor is really an asset."

*Assets are also the qualities, relationships, and experiences everyone needs to be successful in life. These kinds of assets are called **Developmental Assets** because they are the nutrients we all need to develop into healthy, happy, and responsible people. They are positive "building blocks"—relationships, experiences, values, attitudes, and attributes that young people need to be successful in their lives.*

So what are they exactly? Here is the big list of 40 assets! (Distribute Handout 1, 40 Developmental Assets for Adolescents, again.) *I handed this*

out during our first meeting, so I hope you've had a chance to review the assets.

Referring to the list of 40 Developmental Assets, **SAY** *Look at the very first set of assets— SUPPORT! That's right, getting good support from people and providing good support to others is really important in life. You know this because you know how important friends are.*

5 **EXPLAIN** *Turn to a partner and name one person in the school who supports you and tell what this person does to show that support. Students, please talk about an adult in the school. Adults, talk about a student in the school. You have 2 minutes.*

When time is up, **ASK** participants: *Would anyone like to share who you chose and what this person is doing to support you?* (Take several responses.)

Identifying Strength Assets

6 Ask them to look at the list of the 40 Developmental Assets. Briefly explain the categories and touch on some of the assets.

SAY *I would like you to circle three assets that you have and think about why those assets are strong in you. We'll call these your "strength assets."*

Give the participants a few minutes to complete the task. Then ask the participants to get into groups of four. If adults are present, include one in each group.

SAY *In your groups, I would like each of you, one at a time, to share all three of your strength assets and tell why they are strong in you. Any questions?* Allow about 10 minutes.

7 When time is up, **ASK** *Would anyone like to share with the whole group a strength asset you have and tell why you feel this asset is strong in you?* (Take several responses.)

Set an Asset Goal

8 **SAY** *Next, identify and circle one asset that you don't quite have but you would like to acquire. Also, consider what you are going to do to begin to develop that asset.* Allow about 2 minutes for people to do this.

After 2 minutes, **SAY** *In your groups, I would like each of you, one at a time, to share the asset you* want to acquire and tell what you are going to do to begin to reach that goal.

ASK *Any questions?* Give them about 10 minutes to share.

When time is up, **ASK** *Would anyone like to share an asset that you would like to work on and what you plan to do to develop that asset?* (Take several responses.)

9 Distribute Activity Sheet 3, Asset Goal. Briefly explain it and then give participants 8 to 10 minutes to complete their activity sheets.

When time is up, **ASK** *Would someone please share your Asset Goal?* (Take several responses.) Then ask participants to briefly share their asset goals with one other person in the room.

SAY *Your partner should be someone you know and see fairly often. After you have shared your goal, ask your partner to sign your sheet as a witness to your plan. I'd like you to periodically check on your partner's progress in attaining her or his asset goal. Offer support when needed.*

Collect the activity sheets and file them in students' personal folders. **SAY** *In future meetings we will have a chance to look at these again.*

10 **ASK** *What is the point of this activity and what does it have to do with our mission of promoting a more caring and supportive school climate?*

(Knowing about assets is good; building assets in ourselves and others is good; caring and support are assets; we all need support; when we care about or support others, we are strengthening assets in others and ourselves; when we promote assets in others, we are strengthening our own assets; we give and we get; what goes around, comes around; assets are positive norms.)

11 Thank the group for sharing and for making a difference in the school.

Discuss when and where the next meeting will be. If possible, set the time and place now.

Closure

12 Close with the entire group standing in a circle, and **ASK** *Would anyone like to share anything with this group (feelings, thoughts, words of encouragement, etc.)?*

Thank the group for its commitment and willingness to help make the school a better place. Once again, state the date, time, and location of the next meeting.

AND MY GOALS ARE . . .

Alert: The last two areas of Activity Sheet 4 concern the issue of alcohol and other drug use. Be prepared to follow up with any concerns that are expressed by participants. For example, you may need to have a personal conversation with a student or even refer a student to a counselor.

READY

Summary: Participants recognize their personal power to shape their own lives and to affect others in a positive way by setting specific goals in different areas of their lives. They share these goals with one close friend, who will encourage them to pursue their goals for the longer term.

SET

Time Required: 45 minutes

Assets Promoted: Caring School Climate, Community Values Youth, Youth as Resources, Positive Peer Influence, High Expectations, Caring, Personal Power, Restraint, Positive View of Personal Future, Planning and Decision Making

Materials Needed:

List or poster of the 40 Developmental Assets
Activity Sheet 4: And My Goals Are . . .

Display Chart 1: Mission
Display Chart 2: Agreements

Preparation:

- Read the lesson and think about how to facilitate it to meet your group's and school's particular needs. Keep in mind that the scripted parts (shown in italics) of the lesson provide only suggested language. Feel free to modify to fit your own style and your group's unique goals.
- Make copies of Activity Sheet 4 (see pages 120–122), one per participant.
- Display the 40 Developmental Assets, as well as Display Charts 1 and 2, where all participants can see them.

Variation: To give students time to seriously consider their goals for each of the 12 areas on Activity Sheet 4, you may want to cover this lesson in three meetings, addressing four areas in each session. Another option is to cover this lesson in two meetings: In the first meeting, you would introduce the goals and explain Activity Sheet 4; then allow the students to take the sheet home and write their goals for each activity. In the second meeting, students would share their goals. Feel free to extend this lesson in any way that would benefit your students.

GO

Review of Previous Meetings

1 Welcome participants, thank them for being here, and **REMIND** them: *We are here today to continue with our efforts to improve our school. What is our mission?*

Refer to Display Chart 1, Mission, and **SAY** *Our mission is to promote a safer and more supportive school climate, to help build more caring relationships, and to begin to understand the importance of the Developmental Assets.*

ASK *What did we discuss at our last meeting?* (Review.)

Explain that the purpose of ongoing meetings is to remind ourselves of the importance of continuing to make a difference in our school.

Refer to Display Chart 2, Agreements, and give a brief review.

Setting Important Goals

2 **EXPLAIN** *Today we will look at some goals in different areas of our lives. Would any of you like to share a goal that you accomplished or are working toward?* (Take several responses.)

SAY *Goals are important in our lives. Goals are like the rudder and propeller of a ship. They give direction and power. Without them, the ship is likely to drift under the power of the wind, waves, and currents. Without goals, we could be set adrift.*

Referring to the list of 40 Developmental Assets, **SAY** *Goals empower us and are important for developing several assets, including 32—Planning and Decision Making; 37—Personal Power; and 40—Positive View of Personal Future.*

3 **EXPLAIN** *Today we have a handout that will help us define some of our goals in important areas of our lives. Each of the 12 areas on this handout connect to at least one of the eight categories of Developmental Assets.*

Distribute Activity Sheet 4, And My Goals Are . . . **SAY** *Synonyms for the word "goal," as listed under the title, include aim, purpose, hope, and wish.*

ASK *Would anyone like to read the first bulleted point listed under the title, And My Goals Are . . .?* Allow one participant to read the first point, thank that person, then rephrase or make an appropriate comment about the statement, such as, "By making choices, I use my personal power to shape my own life." (Repeat the process until all five points are covered.)

4 Read the directions that follow the last bulleted point. Briefly read through all 12 general areas, pointing out the asset category each one relates to, ask if there are any questions, and, if necessary, explain. Then **SAY** *We will take about 15 minutes to give you all time to work on this handout individually. Read through each area and example carefully; then, for each area, write a personal goal that is real for you. If possible, try to establish goals that are measurable; you want to be able to track your progress toward achieving each goal. For example, I will exercise for 30 minutes every day.*

SAY *When everyone has finished writing, you will find a partner to share your individual goals.*

I would like to remind you again of our agreements, especially confidentiality. It is very important that what we talk about here does not leave this room. What is said here should stay here! Can we agree on that point again? (Reach a consensus of yes.)

Sharing Goals

5 When time is up, ask them to share their plans with their partners. Allow about 10 minutes to do this.

When time is up, **ASK** *Would anyone like to share a goal with the group?* (Take a few responses.)

SAY *We will look at these again in future meetings to check on our progress.*

Collect the activity sheets and file them in participants' personal folders.

6 **ASK** *What is the point of this activity and what does it have to do with our mission of promoting a more caring and supportive school climate?* **(It helps us to become positive role models for others; if we make better choices, it not only helps us but helps others, too; writing goals is a good idea because then we are more likely to accomplish them; some goals directly apply to our mission, such as cultural competence and service to others; it helps us to lead by example, by doing the right thing.)** Take several responses.

7 Thank the group for sharing and for making a difference in the school.

Discuss when and where the next meeting will be. If possible, set the time and place now.

Closure

8 Close with the entire group standing in a circle. **ASK** *Would anyone like to share anything with this group (feelings, thoughts, words of encouragement, etc.)?*

Thank the group for its commitment and willingness to help make the school a better place. Once again, state the date, time, and location of the next meeting.

THE COMMITMENT

Note This lesson can be used after several meetings as a review and as an ongoing personal commitment to make a difference in the school.

READY

Summary: Participants are given an opportunity to review what they learned from the meetings and to create individual lists of what each is willing to do as a result. They share their lists as a commitment to make a difference in the school.

SET

Time Required: 45 minutes

Assets Promoted: Caring School Climate, Community Values Youth, Youth as Resources, Service to Others, High Expectations, Positive Peer Influence, Caring, Honesty, Responsibility, Interpersonal Competence

Materials Needed:

List or poster of the 40 Developmental Assets
Poster board or flip-chart paper
Handout 3: Commitment Card

Display Chart 1: Mission
Display Chart 2: Agreements
Display Chart 8: Discussion Questions #3 and #4

Preparation:

- Read the lesson and think about how to facilitate it to meet your group's and school's particular needs. Keep in mind that the scripted parts (shown in italics) of the lesson provide only suggested language. Feel free to modify to fit your own style and your group's unique goals.
- Make copies of Handout 3 (see pages 97–98), one per participant. Ideally, these should be copied onto 8.5"x 11" paper, two sided and folded in half.
- Make Display Chart 8 (see page 112), using poster board or flip-chart paper.
- Display the 40 Developmental Assets, as well as Display Charts 1, 2, and 8 where all participants can see them.

GO

Review of Previous Meetings

1 Welcome participants, thank them for being here, and REMIND them: *We are here today to continue with our efforts to improve our school. What is our mission?*

Refer to Display Chart 1, Mission, and SAY *Our mission is to promote a safer and more support-* *ive school climate, to help build more caring relationships, and to understand the importance of the Developmental Assets.*

ASK *What did we discuss at our last meeting?* (Review.)

Explain that the purpose of ongoing meetings is to remind ourselves of the importance of continuing to make a difference in our school.

Refer to Display Chart 2, Agreements, and give a brief review.

Memories and Actions

2 **SAY** *Today we are going to give you an opportunity to review what we have done since our first meeting, to create a personal plan, and to make a commitment to continue to foster a more caring climate in our school.*

3 **SAY** *First we will discuss what we have done to make a difference.*

ASK participants to answer the following questions on a sheet of paper.

Refer to Display Chart 8 and read Discussion Questions #3 and #4:
- *What will you remember from our time together and our efforts to make a difference in the school?*
- *What have you done to make a difference in your school?*

Allow 5 to 10 minutes for participants to complete the task.

Small Group Discussions

4 Direct participants to form into groups of four. If adults are present, include one in each group.

SAY *I would like each of you to share the answers to your questions with your small group. We'll take about 10 minutes for this discussion.*

5 When time is up, **ASK** *Would anyone like to share anything that was said in your group?* (Take several responses.)

Make any appropriate comments and thank participants for sharing.

6 **ASK** *Can anyone tell me what the word "commitment" means?* **(Obligation, duty, promise, responsibility.)**

EXPLAIN *Each of us will receive a Commitment Card that will help define our personal commitment to make a difference.* Distribute copies of Handout 3, Commitment Card.

7 Give an overview of the card, showing all four sides. Request that the participants write only on the two inside pages. **SAY** *Anything you write on your card will be shared with others in this room.* (After the activity, you may want to collect the cards to make copies so you can evaluate what participants have learned and what their intentions are. If so, explain that to the group.)

SAY *I would like you to think about all the topics, discussions, thoughts, and feelings shared here, and write what you have learned or will remember on the inside left cover. Then on the right-hand side, write down what your plans and/or intentions are. Any questions?*

Allow the participants about 8 minutes to complete the inside two pages of their cards.

8 When time is up, **SAY** *We will now share our cards with others. Get back into the same groups of four.* Explain that there will be two opportunities to share.

EXPLAIN *Each member of your group should first share only what you've learned or will remember since our first time together when we introduced the mission. Just read the left-hand side of the card. After all participants have shared their answers to the first question, stop; do not read from the right-hand side yet! Any questions? You have about 5 minutes for this discussion.*

When time is up, **ASK** *Would anyone like to share with the entire group what you learned and/or will remember?* (Take several responses.) Thank participants for sharing.

9 **SAY** *Now you may share the commitments on the right-hand side of the card.*

Any questions? You have about 5 minutes to discuss your commitments.

When time is up, **ASK** *Would anyone like to share with the entire group any commitments from your card?* (Take several responses.)

When you are finished, thank the participants and give them time to add anything to their cards, if they wish.

Words of Support

(10) Tell participants to pass their cards around within their small groups. Ask each member to write words of encouragement and support on the back of the card, and then sign their names. (Give examples of what can be written, such as "Thanks for being such a good friend"; "Thank you for being a positive role model"; "Let's remind and help each other to stick to our commitments"; "I admire your courage.")

Ask if there are any questions, and then give them about 8 minutes to write on each other's cards.

(11) When time is up, **SAY** *Later, after we are done, others outside of your small group can write on your card, if you wish. Ask them to read your card before they write on it so that they understand the commitment you're making.*

When everyone is done, collect all the cards. Tell participants that copies of the cards will be made and placed in their personal folders.

SAY *At our next meeting your card will be returned to you. When you get your card, take it home and keep it someplace where you will see it often, like on your nightstand or desk. Your card will remind you of your commitment to continue to make a difference in our school.*

(12) Thank the group for sharing and for making a difference.

Discuss when and where the next meeting will be. If possible, establish the time and place now.

Closure

(13) Close with the entire group standing in a circle. **ASK** *Would anyone like to share anything with this group (feelings, thoughts, words of encouragement, etc.)?*

Thank the group for its commitment and willingness to help make the school a better place. Once again, state the date, time, and location of the next meeting.

TEAM BUILDING

FIGURE THIS OUT!

Tip: During the tennis ball activity, look for examples of participants encouraging and discouraging others so that you'll be prepared for the process questions.

READY

Summary: Participants solve a problem in small groups to promote team building. Participants also gain insight into how they relate to others.

SET

Time Required: 45 minutes

Assets Promoted: Caring School Climate, Youth as Resources, Service to Others, High Expectations, Positive Peer Influence, Bonding to School, Caring, Honesty, Responsibility, Interpersonal Competence

Materials Needed:

List or poster of the 40 Developmental Assets
Display Chart 1: Mission
Display Chart 2: Agreements
Display Chart 9: Figure This Out! (Rules)
Stopwatches or watches with second hand, one per group of eight

Poster board or flip-chart paper
Tennis balls, one per group of eight

Preparation:

- Read the lesson and think about how to facilitate it to meet your group's and school's particular needs. Keep in mind that the scripted parts (shown in italics) of the lesson provide only suggested language. Feel free to modify to fit your own style and your group's unique goals.
- Make Display Chart 9 (see page 113), using poster board or flip-chart paper.
- Display the 40 Developmental Assets, as well as Display Charts 1, 2, and 9, where all participants can see them.

GO

Review of Previous Meetings

(1) Welcome participants, thank them for being here, and **REMIND** them: *We are here today to continue with our efforts to improve our school. What is our mission?*

Refer to Display Chart 1, Mission, and **SAY** *Our mission is to promote a safer and more supportive school climate, to help build more caring relationships, and to understand the importance of the Developmental Assets.*

ASK *What did we discuss at our last meeting?* (Review.)

Explain that the purpose of ongoing meetings is to remind ourselves of the importance of continuing to make a difference in our school.

Refer to Display Chart 2, Agreements, and give a brief review.

2 **SAY** *Today we are going to give you an opportunity to work together as a team to solve a problem. You will also examine and discuss the dynamics of the process of solving the problem.*

Illustration for "Thinking Outside the Box"

3 **SAY** *I have a riddle for you.* Write these numbers on a flip chart or somewhere else where everyone can see them: 8, 5, 4, 9, 1, 7, 6, 3, 2, 0

Then **ASK** *What is the pattern to this number sequence? You really have to think outside the box to get this.* Give them some time to think about it. They can work on it together if they want. **(Answer: The numbers are arranged alphabetically. Most people will not get this because they are thinking in numerical terms rather than alphabetical terms.)**

If someone gets the answer, **SAY** *That's right! Good job of thinking outside the box! That's what everyone will need to do in this next activity!*

If no one gets it after a few minutes, give them the answer. Then **SAY** *This is an example of thinking outside the box. That's what the next activity will require!*

Tennis Ball Challenge

4 Next, you will guide the participants in an activity called Figure This Out! The ultimate objective of this activity is for team members to pass a tennis ball as fast as possible in the order they establish. To get started, arrange participants into groups of eight, and have each group assign one person to be the timer. (That person needs to have a stopwatch or a watch with a second hand.) Ask one group of eight (the demonstration group) to stand in a circle. Give one person (the leader) a tennis ball, and give the group the following instructions:

I'd like you (the leader) to toss the tennis ball across the circle to someone, then have that person toss the ball across the circle to someone else. Continue in that manner until everyone has had a turn, and the last person has possession of the ball. The last person to catch the ball should then toss it back to the first person (the leader) to complete the pattern. Try that now, and remember the order in which each person catches the ball (the established pattern).

When the demonstration group members complete the task, ask them to try it again, tossing the tennis ball in the established pattern. When they are done the second time, ask them to repeat the process and, this time, **to do it as fast as they can.**

When the demonstration is completed and everyone understands the process, ask the groups to start working on the established pattern. Once a team has its established pattern, then it should start working on speed: getting the ball through the established pattern as quickly as possible. Explain that each group will have an opportunity to be timed to see which team can complete the task the fastest.

5 **SAY** *There are some basic rules that every group needs to follow.*

Referring to Display Chart 9, Figure This Out!, read the following:

The tennis ball must clearly pass from person to person in the established pattern. Every person must touch the ball. The tennis ball cannot be suspended, held, or resting anywhere. Timing starts when the ball leaves the first person's hand(s) and ends when the ball arrives in the first person's hand(s) again. These are the only rules.

Note: The rules do not say that participants have to stay in a circle, but don't point that out to participants. If some participants have done this activity before, ask them to be involved but not to contribute their ideas, since they may already know a good strategy.

Give each group leader a tennis ball and let the groups begin.

6 Give participants several minutes to work on moving the tennis ball through the pattern as quickly as possible. Don't give them any hints other than "Think outside the box!"

As you observe the groups, look for examples of students encouraging and discouraging others.

When one group is satisfied that it has done the activity as quickly as possible, allow a few extra minutes for other groups to work on the challenge.

7 When most groups are done, have the group with the fastest time demonstrate its technique for all to see.

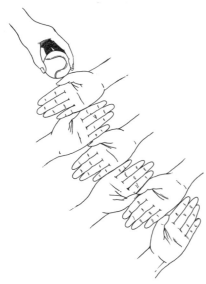

FIGURE 4

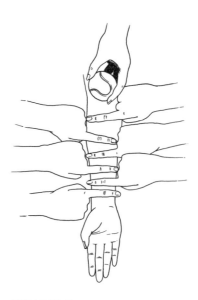

FIGURE 5

Note: One strategy that is very fast begins with group members standing in two lines facing each other. Each person holds out one hand, palm up. All the hands should be held close together (and in the order of the established pattern) to form a "ramp" with a slight incline. The leader releases the ball at the upper end of the ramp and then quickly moves to the lower end to catch it. This takes less than a second! (See Figure 4.)

The fastest-observed strategy again begins with group members standing in two lines facing each other with the leader at the head of and in between the two lines. The leader holds out one arm with the palm up and at a slight incline. Each participant then lays one index finger (in the order of the established pattern) on the leader's forearm. The fingers should be held close together, forming a "ramp" near the leader's wrist. With her or his free hand, the leader releases the ball at the top of the ramp of fingers, and then catches it at the bottom with her or his other hand. This takes less than half a second! (See Figure 5.)

Processing Questions

8 **ASK** the group: *What did we learn from this activity and how does this relate to your mission of promoting a more caring and supportive school climate?* **(It is important to listen; everyone has something to contribute; everyone is important; cooperation is essential; if we remember and**

live by these values, we will be more effective at promoting a more caring school climate.)

9 Then **ASK** *What did you or others do to encourage each other? What did people in your group do to bring out the best in others?* (Take several responses.)

ASK *What did you or others do that may have been discouraging to others?* (Take several responses.)

Close by **SAYING** *It is important to be aware of how we relate to each other and to others in our school. If we truly want to make a difference in our school, it has to start with us and how we interact with others.*

10 Thank the group for sharing and for making a difference.

Discuss when and where the next meeting will be. If possible, establish the time and place now.

Closure

11 Close with the entire group standing in a circle, and **ASK** *Would anyone like to share anything with this group (feelings, thoughts, words of encouragement, etc.)?*

Thank the group for its commitment and willingness to help make the school a better place. Once again, state the date, time, and location of the next meeting.

GETTING TO KNOW YOU

READY

Summary: This lesson provides an opportunity to get to know others in the group better, to give and receive compliments, to bond, and to strengthen the team.

SET

Time Required: 60 minutes

Assets Promoted: Caring School Climate, Community Values Youth, Youth as Resources, Service to Others, High Expectations, Positive Peer Influence, Caring, Honesty, Responsibility, Interpersonal Competence

Materials Needed:
List or poster of the 40 Developmental Assets
Display Chart 1: Mission
Display Chart 2: Agreements

Blank 3" x 5" index cards, four per participant
Flip-chart paper on a stand with markers
Pens or pencils

Preparation:
- Read the lesson and think about how to facilitate it to meet your group's and school's particular needs. Keep in mind that the scripted parts (shown in italics) of the lesson provide only suggested language. Feel free to modify to fit your own style and your group's unique goals.
- Have index cards ready to distribute.
- Prepare to give a sincere compliment to a participating student (see **9**).
- Display the 40 Developmental Assets, as well as Display Charts 1 and 2, where all participants can see them.

GO

Review of Previous Meetings

1 Welcome participants, thank them for being here, and REMIND them: *We are here today to continue with our efforts to improve our school. What is our mission?*

Refer to Display Chart 1, Mission, and SAY *Our mission is to promote a safer and more supportive school climate, to help build more caring relationships, and to understand the importance of the Developmental Assets.*

ASK *What did we discuss at our last meeting?* (Review.)

Explain that the purpose of ongoing meetings is to remind ourselves of the importance of continuing to make a difference in our school.

Refer to Display Chart 2, Agreements, and give a brief review.

2 **SAY** *Today you are going to have an opportunity to get to know each other better, to connect and help strengthen our team.*

ASK *Have you ever heard the phrase "walk your talk"? What does that mean?* **(Say what you do; mean what you say; practice what you preach.)**

EXPLAIN *If we are truly going to make a difference in our school, it has to begin with this group of people right here. If we are going to be successful in promoting a more caring and supportive school climate, we have to be caring and supportive of each other. When we have an opportunity to get to know someone better, we tend to care more about that person. So today we are going to get to know each other better!*

Activity to Learn about Others

3 Pass out an index card to each person. Be sure everyone has a pen or pencil.

Tell participants that they will be putting a great deal of information on this card, so they should not make their letters too large. Also, have them orient their card horizontally (landscape), not vertically (portrait).

SAY *You will share what you write on these cards with the group, so don't write anything you wouldn't be comfortable sharing.*

ASK them to write the following on their index cards. (Do not prepare the chart in advance. As you tell them what to write on their cards, write an example of each item on chart paper or erasable board.)

- *In the center of the card, write #1 and your name.*
- *In the upper left-hand corner of the card, write #2 and the sport you most enjoy playing.*
- *In the upper right-hand corner of the card, write #3 and your favorite place to be (inside or outside).*
- *In the lower left-hand corner of the card, write #4 and the name of someone significant in your life (parent, grandparent, aunt, uncle, sibling, etc.).*
- *In the lower right-hand corner of the card, write #5 and something positive about yourself (friendly, dependable, etc.).*
- *Below your name, write #6 and the name of a famous person in history that you most admire (you don't need to write out why, but be prepared to talk about that).*

- *Near the top of the back of the card, write #7 and something you are proud of (an accomplishment, a kind deed, hard work, etc.).*
- *Under #7, write #8 and an important goal you have in your life.*
- *Under #8, write #9 and the name of someone younger than you, who looks up to you as a role model.*

Optional or substitute categories may include:
- *Write down one of your strength assets, or an asset that you definitely have.*
- *Write down one asset that you don't have but would like to acquire.*

ASK *Any questions?*

4 When everyone has finished writing, demonstrate the remainder of the activity, first by choosing a partner. With your partner, **EXPLAIN** to the group: *I will share all nine categories that I have written on my card with my partner. My partner will listen carefully and may ask questions about anything that isn't clear.*

SAY *When I am done, my partner will share her or his card with me. I will listen attentively and try to remember as much as possible. I, too, may ask questions for clarification.*

When we are done, we stay together and find another pair. This time I introduce my partner to the other pair from memory. I can use my card to help cue me, but I should not look at my partner's card. If I can't remember a point, my partner will help me. Then my partner will introduce me and, finally, the other pair will do the same. When we are all done, the partners stay together and search out a different pair and repeat the process.

ASK *Any questions?*

5 Ask participants to stand up and find someone they don't know very well to be their partner. Recommend that adults pair with students. After everyone has a partner, tell the group members they have about 8 minutes to do all the introductions and then have them begin.

6 When time is up, ask participants to form groups of four, consisting of their partner and the last pair they were with.

7 **ASK** *Would any of you like to share what you learned that was particularly interesting about others in the room?* (Take several responses.)

Then **ASK** *What is the point of this activity and what does it have to do with our mission statement?* **(To help create a more caring and supportive school, we need to create a caring and supportive group; getting to know each other better helps us to be more supportive of each other.)**

Kind Words Activity

8 **SAY** *It seems that many of us find it so easy and natural to complain, criticize, put down, walk away from, or ignore someone, especially when that person is doing something that irritates us. We seem to have little patience or tolerance for people, even those we care about!*

EXPLAIN *For this next activity we are going to look for and bring out the best in others. We are going to begin with those in our group.* Request that the groups of four stay together, take their chairs, and find a place in the room far enough away from other groups so as not to overhear what they are saying. Ask that they sit so that they can see everyone in their group.

9 Give an example of a sincere compliment directed toward a student in the large group. Give another example of a sincere compliment directed toward a student or adult in the group.

EXPLAIN *Each of us will now have the opportunity to directly compliment others in our group. In general, what kind of compliments might we want to give others?* **(Honest; kind; pointing out positive qualities, personality traits, achievements.)**

Suggest that for this activity we emphasize the inside (positive qualities, personality traits) not the outside (physical features, clothing, etc.).

EXPLAIN *Each of you will get three index cards. On each index card please write the name of one member of your group. Write a different name on each of the three cards. Next, write two or three compliments about each person on her or his card. Be as specific as possible with your compliments.* Give an example.

SAY *When you are done, each of you will have an opportunity to share your compliments with the others in your group. You will also give each person the index card that you wrote her or his compliments on.*

ASK *Any questions?*

Give the group 6 to 8 minutes to complete writing.

10 When time is up, **EXPLAIN** *Now you will have an opportunity to give and receive your compliments.* Use one group as an example to explain the process. **SAY** *In each group, one person at a time is the receiver of compliments* (point to one person in the example group). *For example, (name of student) will be the receiver in this group. Each person in the group, one at a time, will give compliments directly to (name of student). All three in the group will share their compliments with (name of student) before moving on to the next receiver. Also, be sure to use the pronoun "you," not "he" or "she," when you are saying the compliments. Speak directly to the person you are complimenting.*

ASK *Any questions?*

11 **EXPLAIN** *When you receive compliments from someone, please acknowledge that person with a "thank you." After the three members of the group have given their compliments to one member, please hand that person the index cards.*

Have the groups continue with the activity. Move around the room to be sure all groups are on task.

12 When everyone is done, **ASK** *How did it feel to receive your compliments?* (Take several responses.) Then **ASK** *How did it feel to give others compliments?* (Again, take several responses.)

Then **ASK** *What is the point of this activity and what does it have to do with our mission of helping to create a more caring and supportive school climate?* **(It's good to give and receive compliments; it is good to acknowledge positive acts; giving compliments is better than putting people down; we feel better when we give compliments; when we give compliments, the person feels cared for and supported; giving compliments can contribute to helping to create a more supportive school climate.)**

13 **ASK** *What can we take from this activity and how can we apply it to our mission?* **(If we make it a point to give compliments to others every day it will have a positive effect on the school's climate.)**

Remind participants to look for opportunities to give compliments.

14 Thank the group for sharing and for making a difference.

Discuss when and where the next meeting will be. If possible, establish the time and place now.

Closure

15 Close with the entire group standing in a circle, and **ASK** *Would anyone like to share anything with this group (feelings, thoughts, words of encouragement, etc.)?*

Thank the group for its commitment and willingness to help make the school a better place. Once again, state the date, time, and location of the next meeting.

TANGLED

Tip: Be prepared to look for examples of participants encouraging and discouraging others during the exercise so that you are prepared for the process questions.

READY

Summary: This lesson provides an opportunity to solve a problem in small groups to promote team building. Participants also gain insight into how they relate to others.

SET

Time Required: 20 minutes

Assets Promoted: Caring School Climate, Youth as Resources, Service to Others, High Expectations, Positive Peer Influence, Bonding to School, Caring, Honesty, Responsibility, Interpersonal Competence

Materials Needed:

List or poster of the 40 Developmental Assets
Display Chart 1: Mission

Display Chart 2: Agreements

Preparation:

- Read the lesson and think about how to facilitate it to meet your group's and school's particular needs. Keep in mind that the scripted parts (shown in italics) of the lesson provide only suggested language. Feel free to modify to fit your own style and your group's unique goals.
- Display the 40 Developmental Assets, as well as Display Charts 1 and 2, where all participants can see them.

GO

Review of Previous Meetings

1 Welcome participants, thank them for being here, and **REMIND** them: *We are here today to continue with our efforts to improve our school. What is our mission?*

Refer to Display Chart 1, Mission, and **SAY** *Our mission is to promote a safer and more supportive school climate, to help build more caring relationships, and to understand the importance of the Developmental Assets.*

ASK *What did we discuss at our last meeting?* (Review.)

Explain that the purpose of ongoing meetings is to remind ourselves of the importance of continuing to make a difference in our school.

Refer to Display Chart 2, Agreements, and give a brief review.

Small Group Activity

2 **SAY** *Today we are going to give you an opportunity to work together as a team to solve a problem. You will also examine and discuss the dynamics of the process of solving the problem.*

3 Arrange participants into groups of seven or eight (six is too few, nine too many). Ask that each of the groups stand in a circle. Also ask that the groups space themselves apart from the other groups.

4 Ask participants to raise their right hands and reach across their group to shake someone else's hand. **SAY** *Hold on to that hand and do not let go! Raise your left hand and reach across and shake someone else's hand. Do not let go!*

5 Explain that the task is to untangle themselves without letting go of any hands. **SAY** *You can change the position of your hands, so you don't twist your arm or wrist, but you cannot break your connection. Any questions?*

6 Give participants several minutes to solve this problem. Also, as you are observing the groups, look for examples of participants encouraging or discouraging others.

When one group has solved the problem, allow a few extra minutes for other groups to get untangled.

7 When all groups are untangled (or you need to move on for the sake of time), **ASK** *What did you or others do to encourage each other? What did people in your group do to bring out the best in others?* (Take several responses.)

Then **ASK** *What did you or others do to discourage each other?* (Take several responses.)

Close by **SAYING** *It is important to be aware of how we relate to each other and others in our school. If we truly want to make a difference in our school, it has to start with us and how we interact with others.*

8 Finally, **ASK** the group: *What did we learn from this activity and how does this relate to your mission of promoting a more caring and supportive school climate?* **(It is important to listen; everyone has something to contribute; everyone is important; cooperation is essential; if we do all these things, we will be more effective at promoting a more caring school climate.)**

9 Thank the group for sharing and for making a difference.

Discuss when and where the next meeting will be. If possible, set the time and place now.

Closure

10 Close with the entire group standing in a circle, and **ASK** *Would anyone like to share anything with this group (feelings, thoughts, words of encouragement, etc.)?*

Thank the group for its commitment and willingness to help make the school a better place. Once again, state the date, time, and location of the next meeting.

SCHOOL ENGAGEMENT

ASSETIZE THIS!

Note: Make sure to present Lesson 4 prior to this lesson.

Students may share sensitive information during this lesson and the assignment. Emphasize confidentiality, and make sure your students understand the importance of keeping information confidential.

READY

Summary: Participants share the asset message by presenting an exercise to their peers. Participants explain the 40 Developmental Assets, then help their friends to identify two strength assets and one asset goal. Participants then help their friends to develop an implementation plan to achieve that asset goal.

SET

Time Required: 30 minutes

Assets Promoted: Varies, depending on the assets on which each individual chooses to focus.

Materials Needed:

List or poster of the 40 Developmental Assets
Display Chart 1: Mission
Display Chart 2: Agreements

Activity Sheet 5: My Assets/My Goal
Handout 1: 40 Developmental Assets for Adolescents

Preparation:

- Read the lesson and think about how to facilitate it to meet your group's and school's particular needs. Keep in mind that the scripted parts (shown in italics) of the lesson provide only suggested language. Feel free to modify to fit your own style and your group's unique goals.
- Make copies of Handout 1 (see pages 94–95) and Activity Sheet 5 (see pages 123–124), three of each per participant.
- Prepare to share with the group real-life examples of what you are doing to promote assets in the lives of two young people (see **4**).
- Display the 40 Developmental Assets, as well as Display Charts 1 and 2, where all participants can see them.

GO

Review of Previous Meetings

1 Welcome participants, thank them for being here, and **REMIND** them: *We are here today to continue with our efforts to improve our school. What is our mission?*

Refer to Display Chart 1, Mission, and **SAY** *Our mission is to promote a safer and more supportive school climate, to help build more caring relationships, and to understand the importance of the Developmental Assets.*

ASK *What did we discuss at our last meeting?* (Review.)

Explain that the purpose of ongoing meetings is to remind ourselves of the importance of continuing to make a difference in our school.

Refer to Display Chart 2, Agreements, and give a brief review.

Review of the Developmental Assets

2 **SAY** *Today we are going to continue our work with the 40 Developmental Assets.*

ASK *Can anyone tell me what the 40 Developmental Assets are?* (**They are positive "building blocks"—relationships, experiences, values, attitudes, and attributes that young people need to be successful in their lives.**)

SAY *We are going to review the 40 Developmental Assets and think about how we might share the asset message and promote these assets for others.*

3 Distribute Handout 1, 40 Developmental Assets for Adolescents. Briefly review the categories and mention a few of the assets.

4 Choose one asset, define it, and briefly explain why you think this asset is important for the health and well-being of a young person. Give an example of what you are personally doing to promote that particular asset in the life of a young person.

Choose another asset, define it, and briefly explain why you think this asset is important for the health and well-being of a young person. Give an example of what you are personally doing to promote that particular asset in the life of another young person.

What Assets Would Benefit My Friends?

5 **SAY** *I would like you once again to look over the list of 40 assets. As you are reading over the list, I would like you to think about which assets would benefit your friends and why.*

SAY *Turn to a partner or a pair and name those assets that your friends would benefit from, and say*

why. Please do not say your friends' names. Instead of using names, you might consider saying, "My friends could benefit from . . ." (or "I know someone who would benefit from . . .")

ASK *Any questions?* Allow participants about 5 minutes to discuss the topic.

When time is up, **ASK** *Which assets do you feel your friends could benefit from and why?* (Take several responses.)

6 **SAY** *We want to spread the asset message to other students, beginning with our friends.*

Distribute Activity Sheet 5, My Strength Assets/ My Goal.

EXPLAIN *You may recall that we previously did a similar activity, Go for 40. Today we are going to use this handout as a tool to share the Developmental Assets with friends and help your friends identify their assets.*

EXPLAIN *I would like to remind you again of our agreements, especially confidentiality. It is very important that what you talk about during this exercise stay between you and your friend. We need to do this activity in confidence.*

Remember, we have a purpose for being here. We are here to promote a more supportive school. We are counting on you all to make this happen! Can we handle this? Can we hold to the agreement of confidentiality? (Reach an affirmative consensus.)

7 **SAY** *Please look at your handout, My Assets My Goal. Would someone please read the first paragraph?*

When the student is done reading, **SAY** *When you approach your friend about this exercise, first let her or him know what you are doing and then ask for permission to talk about Developmental Assets. Help your friend feel comfortable in terms of privacy and the confidentiality of this process.*

ASK *Would someone please read the second paragraph?*
Can someone give me an example of an asset that is based upon a relationship? (assets 1–6, 14)
Can someone give me an example of an asset that is based upon an experience? (7–20, 23, 25, 32)
Can someone give me an example of an asset that is based upon a value or attitude? (21–40)

8 ASK *Would someone please read the third paragraph?* When the student is done reading, SAY *With your partner, I would like you to use this handout as a tool to identify two of your partner's strength assets. One person plays the role of presenter while the other is doing the exercise. Each of you will have an opportunity to do both. Please choose who will be the first presenter now.*

EXPLAIN *Presenter, you will begin from the top. Read the paragraph again to your partner, and then, as the directions say, both of you look at the list of the 40 assets. Help your partner identify what her or his strength assets are and why. Have your partner fill in the blanks on the handout. Your role as presenter is to ask questions and then to help your friend clarify her or his answers. Your job is not to provide answers for your friend.*

We will take about 8 minutes for this activity. When the first person is done filling out the form, switch roles so your partner can complete the form. Repeat the same process.

Any questions? As students begin the activity, monitor their progress and answer any questions that arise.

When time is up, ASK *Would any of you like to share one of your strength assets and why it is a strength?* (Take several responses.)

9 ASK *Would someone please read the paragraph introducing Part 2 (My Asset Goal)?* When the student is done reading, say: *With your same partner, take your original roles as presenter and the person doing the exercise. Presenter, read the same paragraph to your partner. Again, presenter, help your partner identify the asset he or she wants to build, and help to clarify what he or she will do to promote that asset. The partners doing the exercise will again fill in the blanks on their own handout. When you are done, be sure you sign and date the handout. After both of you have signed, switch roles again and repeat the process. Any questions? You have about 6 minutes.*

When time is up, ASK *Would any of you like to share your asset goal and what you plan to do to promote that asset in yourself?* (Take several responses.)

SAY *We will look at these again in future meetings to check on our progress.*

Collect the handouts, file them in the students' personal folders, and plan a review in future meetings.

Sharing the Asset Message in School

10 SAY *Now we are going to share the asset message with our friends!*

Distribute Activity Sheet 5, My Assets/My Goal (two per participant) and Handout 1, 40 Developmental Assets for Adolescents (two per participant).

EXPLAIN *All of you will get two copies of each handout. The goal is for you to present the exercise to at least two of your friends. As the presenter, you will go through the same process we went through here, questioning, probing, clarifying, and defining both the strength assets and the asset goal.*

The first thing you will need to do is to decide who you will ask to do the exercise. Who might you ask? **(Friends, classmates, etc.)** *Then you will need to arrange a time and place to meet that is convenient for both of you. When is a good time?* **(When there are few distractions.)** *Where is a good place?* **(Seated at a table in a quiet area.)** *The exercise will probably take a maximum of 30 minutes to complete.*

When you meet, read the first paragraph on the My Assets/My Goal sheet, and then ask whether your friend feels comfortable about doing the exercise.

After you are done with the exercise, what's the next step? **(Be sure you both sign the sheet, thank the person, give both handouts to your friend, ask her or him to refer to them from time to time.)**

SAY *Finally, the last thing you might say is: "I am going to check with you from time to time to see if you are still working toward your goal and whether there is anything I can do to help."*

ASK *Any questions, comments, or concerns?*

11 ASK *What is the point of this activity and what does it have to do with our mission of promoting a more caring and supportive school climate?* **(Assets are important for everyone; building assets for and with others is good; caring and support are assets; we all need support; when we care about or support others, we are strengthening assets for others and for ourselves; when we promote assets in others, we are strengthening our own assets; we give and we get; what goes around, comes around; assets are positive norms.)**

12 Thank the group for sharing and for making a difference in the school.

Discuss when and where the next meeting will be. If possible, establish the time and place now.

Closure

13 Close with the entire group standing in a circle, and ASK *Would anyone like to share anything with this group (feelings, thoughts, words of encouragement, etc.)?*

Thank the group for its commitment and willingness to help make the school a better place. Once again, state the date, time, and location of the next meeting.

IT PAYS TO BE KIND

READY

Summary: The purpose of this lesson is to recognize, thank, and reward students and staff members in the school who offer acts of kindness toward others. It also requests that they wear their reward as a reminder to always be kind to others.

SET

Time Required: 30 minutes

Assets Promoted: Caring School Climate, Community Values Youth, Youth as Resources, Service to Others, High Expectations, Positive Peer Influence, Caring, Honesty, Responsibility, Interpersonal Competence

Materials Needed:

List or poster of the 40 Developmental Assets
Handout 4: Kindness Recognition Cards, at least three per person
Activity Sheet 6: *It Pays to Be Kind* Log

Display Chart 1: Mission
Display Chart 2: Agreements

Optional: Wristbands that say *No act of kindness, no matter how small, is ever wasted,* at least three per person. (Other options for kindness rewards/reminders are a leather cord bracelet, safety pin with beads, ribbon, friendship bracelet, or some other creative token that participants can make. You could also simply give the Kindness Recognition Cards.)

Preparation:

- Read the lesson and think about how to facilitate it to meet your group's and school's particular needs. Keep in mind that the scripted parts (shown in italics) of the lesson provide only suggested language. Feel free to modify to fit your own style and your group's unique goals.
- Make copies of Activity Sheet 6 (see page 125), at least one per participant.
- Be prepared to share at least one act of kindness that you observed in your school, offered by one student to another (see **2**).
- Be prepared to give sincere recognition and thanks to a participant for a kind act he or she offered someone in the school (see **5** below).
- If you plan to distribute the "Kindness" wristbands, make sure you have ordered and received them (see page 9 for ordering information). If you are going to make your own kindness reward, make sure you have the materials to do that.
- Make copies of Handout 4 (see page 99) on colored card stock (or laminate the cards). Cut out individual cards so they easily fit into the plastic bags containing the wristbands.
- If you are distributing the wristbands, insert one card with each wristband so that the writing is visible from the outside of the bag. (Note: This can be done prior to the meeting or can be incorporated into the activity in Lesson 11.)
- Display the 40 Developmental Assets, as well as Display Charts 1 and 2, where all participants can see them.

GO

Review of Previous Meetings

1 Welcome participants, thank them for being here, and **REMIND** them: *We are here today to continue with our efforts to improve our school. What is our mission?*

Refer to Display Chart 1, Mission, and **SAY** *Our mission is to promote a safer and more supportive school climate, to help build more caring relationships, and to understand the importance of the Developmental Assets.*

ASK *What did we discuss at our last meeting?* (Review.)

Explain that the purpose of ongoing meetings is to remind ourselves of the importance of continuing to make a difference in our school.

Refer to Display Chart 2, Agreements, and give a brief review.

Noticing Acts of Kindness

2 **SAY** *Today we are going to focus on kind acts and promoting kindness in the school.* Give an example of a student's kind act that you observed in your school.

ASK *What kind acts, offered by students or adults, have you observed in school this year? Turn to a partner or a pair and share.* After about 3 minutes, ask the students to share in the large group.

3 When time is up, **ASK** all participants: *What kind acts, offered by students or adults, have you observed in this school this year?* (Take several responses.)

Then **ASK** those who shared the kind acts they observed: *What did you do after you observed the act of kindness?*

4 **ASK** *What should we do when we see someone doing something kind toward others? Maybe it's a good idea to recognize, acknowledge, and thank the person for being kind. For example: "Kimberly, it was really kind of you to help Jessie pick up her books after they fell. Thank you for doing that!"*

ASK *Why should we acknowledge those who are kind toward others?* **(It tends to encourage people to do more kind acts; it can inspire others to be kind.)**

Spread the Kindness

5 Enthusiastically state: *Here's our plan!* Introduce the reward by modeling this activity.

Recognize one participant for a kind act that he or she offered another person. *For example, I saw David helping Chad clean up after he dropped his lunch tray. That was a really nice thing for you to do. Because of your kindness, I want to thank you and to give you this.*

Then give the reward (with the Kindness Recognition Card). **ASK** the recipient to read the card to the group, as follows:

No act of kindness, no matter how small, is ever wasted. *Our group is helping to create a more caring school. We are recognizing those students and staff who are kind and caring. You have received this reward because of a kind act that you offered others. Please wear it as a token of our appreciation and as a gentle reminder for you to continue to show your kindness.* ***Thank you for what you have done!***

If rewards were not given to each participant earlier, pass one out to each participant. Or pass out materials for each person to make rewards. **SAY** *We want each of you to have this as a reminder for you to be kind as well.*

6 **SAY** *Each of you will be given three kindness rewards. Each kindness reward will have a card with the message I just shared. Your mission is the following:*
- *Look for acts of kindness offered by students or staff;*
- *Recognize and thank the person for being kind by presenting her or him with a reward and/or Kindness Recognition Card; and*
- *Encourage that person to do more acts of kindness.*

It is important to recognize the kind act as soon as possible after you observe it. That way, it will have more impact on the person you are recognizing. Are there any questions?

7 **ASK** *Do we want to give these rewards to our friends? Of course—but only if our friends earn it by being kind to another person! This is important to keep the value, meaning, and integrity of this activity. If we give these rewards to friends just because they are friends, that will weaken the meaning, power, and significance of the activity.*

8 **ASK** *Should we broadcast this activity to all?* Reach the consensus that doing this activity without publicity reinforces the true meaning and significance.

9 As you distribute Activity Sheet 6, *It Pays to Be Kind* Log, three rewards, and three Recognition Cards to each participant, **SAY** *Make a note on the log of the people you recognized and what they did. Each of you will receive three rewards now to distribute in the school.*

(Optional) **EXPLAIN** *If you give all three away, bring your log to me. I will file it in your personal folder and give you a new log and three more rewards and Recognition Cards. Any comments or questions?*

SUGGESTION: Collect the logs and in future meetings discuss them with the intention of publicly recognizing students who have been especially kind to others.

Recognition can be given, for example, during an all-school assembly.

Discuss when and where the next meeting will be. If possible, establish the time and place now.

Closure

10 Close with the entire group standing in a circle, and **ASK** *Would anyone like to share anything with this group (feelings, thoughts, words of encouragement, etc.)?*

Thank the group for its commitment and willingness to help make the school a better place. Once again, state the date, time, and location of the next meeting.

QUIET CONNECTIONS

Alert: : Because potentially sensitive information could be shared, you'll want to give some extra thought to this lesson before you present it. If you feel your students cannot do this activity in confidence, in a genuinely caring way, or that they are not mature enough to handle it, please modify it so that the objectives are met. Suggestions include not naming names; not discussing the specific situations of students who participants feel need support; and holding discussions only between individual students and adults, one-on-one.

*The intent of this lesson is to have participants write weekly entries into their logs for a long term (12 weeks). This can be a powerful and significant lesson. However, there are some logistical and time commitments involved with this activity. **An adult should facilitate this lesson.***

READY

Summary: This lesson identifies students who could benefit from some extra support. Participants are challenged to intentionally offer support to one student they have identified. They create a plan to facilitate the offer of support for that person.

SET

Time Required: 60 minutes

Assets Promoted: Caring School Climate, Community Values Youth, Youth as Resources, Positive Peer Influence, Caring, Responsibility, Interpersonal Competence

Materials Needed:
List or poster of the 40 Developmental Assets
Display Chart 1: Mission
Display Chart 2: Agreements

Activity Sheet 7: *Quiet Connections* Log
Blank 3" x 5" index cards, one per person

Preparation:
- Read the lesson and think about how to facilitate it to meet your group's and school's particular needs. Keep in mind that the scripted parts (shown in italics) of the lesson provide only suggested language. Feel free to modify to fit your own style and your group's unique goals.
- Make copies of Activity Sheet 7 (see pages 126–127), one per participant.
- Before the session, select three students to demonstrate the support fall (see ❸).
- Have index cards ready to distribute.
- Display the 40 Developmental Assets, as well as Display Charts 1 and 2, where all participants can see them.

GO

Review of Previous Meetings

❶ Welcome participants, thank them for being here, and REMIND them: *We are here today to continue with our efforts to improve our school. What is our mission?*

Refer to Display Chart 1, Mission, and
SAY *Our mission is to promote a safer and more supportive school climate, to help build more caring*

relationships, and to understand the importance of the Developmental Assets.

ASK *What did we discuss at our last meeting?* (Review.)

Explain that the purpose of ongoing meetings is to remind ourselves of the importance of continuing to make a difference in our school.

Refer to Display Chart 2, Agreements, and give a brief review.

Demonstrating Support

2 **SAY** *Today, we are going to give you an opportunity to identify a student in the school who would benefit from a little extra support and then to give her or him that support.*

3 Explain to the participants that three volunteers were asked to demonstrate what support looks like in simple terms. Ask the three volunteers to come forward to demonstrate the trust fall. **SAY** *As you probably recall, we did this exercise in a previous session.*

Align volunteers in front of the room so all can see. If necessary, describe the activity to the group by explaining that one person will fall into the hands of the two supporters. Say that the volunteer faller will depend upon the supporters for her or his physical safety.

Ask the faller to stand upright and rigid with arms folded.

Ask that the supporters stand about two feet directly behind the faller ready to support the person.

Explain the calls (without the volunteers actually moving) as follows:
Faller: My name is (first name) and I am ready for a challenge!
Supporters: We're here for you, (faller's name)!
Faller: Are you ready to support me?
Supporters: Yes!
Faller: Falling!
Supporters: Fall away!

Once you have explained the calls and all the volunteers understand what they are supposed to do, then have the volunteers do their calls with the faller actually falling back, and the supporters catching her or him. The faller needs to fall only about 10 inches to demonstrate the result. Stand

by the faller and coach all the volunteers through the calls. Be close to ensure the safety of the faller and the supporters.

After the demonstration, thank the volunteers and ask for applause for their efforts. **EXPLAIN** *This is what support looks like in simple terms.*

4 **ASK** the faller: *How did it feel to fall and have your friends here to support you?* **(It's a good feeling; I feel secure and safe when I have people supporting me; I feel like I can try to do anything because I know there are people who care about me who are going to be there to catch me if I make a mistake.)**

Demonstrating Lack of True Support

5 Ask the two supporters to **take three steps back** and then ask them to repeat the support fall. Tell the volunteers they will go through the same process, including the calls and responses, but this time the faller will not fall.

6 After the volunteers repeat the process, without the faller falling, **ASK** the faller: *How did it feel this time as opposed to the last time?* **(Scary because I felt little support; I felt they were just saying they would support me, but it was hard to believe because they weren't really close enough to catch me.)**

7 **SAY** *We are going to do this one more time.* Tell supporters: *Stay three steps back, but this time I would like you both to turn your backs to the faller and not respond to the faller's calls. Do not utter a word!*

Tell the faller, once again, not to actually fall, but only to vocalize the calls.

8 Immediately after the volunteers repeat this process, without the faller falling, **ASK** the group: *Are there people in our school who are like (faller's name), that if they fell they would have little or no support?*

Without taking any responses (with the exception of nods or a yes), **ASK** *Are there people in our school who are outcasts or are isolated, excluded, alienated, ignored, or teased?*

Again, without taking any responses (except nods or a yes), **ASK** *Are there people in our school* *like this?* (Without much discussion, come to the consensus of yes.)

Offering Support to Someone Who Needs It

9 **SAY** *Think about one person you know who is like this, who has little or no support or who may be isolated, ignored, or teased. I would like you to write this person's name down on an index card.* (Pass out the cards. Quietly, thank the three volunteers and ask them to be seated.)

Then **SAY** *Under the person's name, I would like you to write down what you are willing to do, even if it's in a small way, to offer that person some support. I am not asking you to become best friends with that person, only to offer some care and support. Any questions?*

If it is appropriate, tell participants: *Also, we will share these cards in small groups when we are done.* (If you feel you need to modify this lesson because of confidentiality concerns, see the note at the beginning of this lesson.)

10 Before participants begin their task, **EXPLAIN** *There is a purpose for doing this activity. Remember, our mission is to help promote a more caring and supportive school for all. In every school there are students who are on the margins, and we would like to see them included.*

11 Referring to Display Chart 2, Agreements, **SAY** *I would like to remind you of a particular word that was mentioned earlier under the heading Respect. That word was "confidentiality." What does "confidentiality" mean?* **(What is said here stays here.)**

SAY *Remember, there is a reason and a purpose for your being here. We see you as leaders in the school. We see you as mature, responsible individuals who can handle doing something like this without talking to others (outside this group), gossiping, or joking about it.*

12 **ASK** *Can we all handle this discussion? Can we take this seriously? If the response is generally positive, continue with the lesson.* (If the response is not positive, and/or you have concerns about confidentiality, see the note at the beginning of this lesson for suggestions on how to modify the lesson.)

Form participants into groups of about six (if any adults are participants, assign one to each group). Have each group sit together in a circle and spread out around the room so as not to distract other groups.

Check on each group to be sure it is on task. Then, if possible, join one group for the discussion. Allow the groups 10 to 15 minutes to complete the task.

13 When time is up, **ASK** *Would anyone like to share any thoughts with the group—anything you realized, learned, or discussed in your group?* (Take several responses.)

14 **EXPLAIN** *Offering support to others is a good thing. We need to be empathetic and act to help others, especially those who have little support. Remember, what goes around, comes around.*

ASK *What if you offer support by saying hi or smiling, and the person's response seems to be "Leave me alone!" or "What's wrong with you?" What should you do if your offer of support is rejected?* **(Back off; leave the person alone; try not to be offended or hurt.)**

ASK *Why do you think people would reject a sincere offer of support?* **(They have been hurt by others in the past; they are defensive; they don't trust anyone; they don't know how to respond appropriately.)**

EXPLAIN *Please keep in mind that what you are doing won't necessarily be easy. You are reaching out to others, but you can't control their reactions. If you are rejected, remember that it is not about you. You are doing a good thing. Some people have been so hurt and isolated that they automatically reject others because they fear being hurt again. Just keep trying to reach them in small ways and hope they will come to see that you have good intentions. I am also available if you need to talk about your efforts or if you have any concerns about anything related to what we are doing here.*

ASK *Are there any questions, comments, or concerns?*

15 **SAY** *We call this activity Quiet Connections. That is because we need to reach out in a quiet way to people we think need support. We need to be careful about how we do this. Think about how the person you want to support would feel if he or she* *thought you were being friendly only because of an assignment or because you see them as an outcast. So make sure you are genuine in your support. You need to reach out to someone because you really care, not because I'm asking you to do this. If your friends ask why you are spending time with someone you normally don't, try saying something like this: "I'm part of a group that is trying to make our school a more caring place. I want Susie to know that I care about her and I want her to feel supported at school." Only talk about it if someone asks you about it. Don't tell people you are spending time with an outcast because you were assigned to do so. If the person you're trying to support heard that, he or she would feel it is not genuine and could be very hurt.*

ASK *Is it okay to tell our friends things we learn about the person we are reaching out to? Can we just tell a few close friends?* (Reach a consensus that it is mandatory not to say anything about the person's specific situation to anyone outside of the group.)

SAY *In addition to reaching out in a genuine way, we need to respect the privacy of the individual. You must maintain complete confidentiality of any personal information he or she may tell you. If you don't feel you can do this in a genuine way and that you can maintain the person's confidentiality, then please refrain from this activity. So, can we all do this in a genuine, confidential way because we really care about creating a supportive school for all students?* (Reach a consensus of yes.)

16 SAY *The last thing we need to do before we close is to think about accountability. Are we doing what we say we are going to do?*

EXPLAIN *I am going to pass out the Quiet Connections Logs. These logs are only between you and me. I want and need to see what you are doing and how often.*

17 Pass out a copy of Activity Sheet 7, *Quiet Connections* Log, to each participant. **SAY** *Please fill out Part 1 of the log and return it to me when you are done.*

EXPLAIN *I will place your Quiet Connections Logs in your personal folders in a file in my office (or other designated place). Your personal folder will be labeled with your name. I would like each of you*

to come to my office to check in once a week. When you're there, make a note on your log of what you have done, in a quiet way, to support the person you said you would support.

Also, notice that 12 weeks are listed on your log. Our goal is to follow this out at least that far. At that point, I would like to sit down with you to review what you have done and to acknowledge your kind and caring efforts. I would also like you to write down your thoughts about your experience in Part 3 of the log. (Note: Reviewing all students' logs will take a lot of time, so before you make this statement, make sure you have the time or that you can share this task with other adults.)

18 Once again **ASK** *Can we handle this? Can we do this and keep it confidential? Any questions?*

Give the participants several minutes to complete their task. Then collect the papers.

19 ASK *What is the point of this activity and what does it have to do with our mission of helping to create a more caring and supportive school climate?* **(We can accomplish our mission of creating a supportive school climate only if we intentionally support all students by reaching out to those who may not be feeling supported at school; by supporting others, we are helping build their assets, as well as our own; we need to look for opportunities to include others.)**

20 Thank the group for sharing and for making a difference.

Discuss when and where the next meeting will be. If possible, establish the time and place now.

Closure

21 Close with the entire group standing in a circle, and **ASK** *Would anyone like to share anything with this group (feelings, thoughts, words of encouragement, etc.)?*

Thank the group for its commitment and willingness to help make the school a better place. Once again, state the date, time, and location of the next meeting.

CHANGING THE NORMS

Note: Make sure you present Lesson 3 prior to presenting this lesson.

READY

Summary: Participants administer a survey to their friends to clarify personal norms. Participants then challenge their friends to join their movement by adopting positive norms and discouraging negative norms in their everyday life.

SET

Time Required: 45 minutes

Assets Promoted: Caring School Climate, Community Values Youth, Youth as Resources, Service to Others, High Expectations, Positive Peer Influence, Caring, Honesty, Responsibility, Interpersonal Competence, Sense of Purpose

Materials Needed:

List or poster of the 40 Developmental Assets
Activity Sheet 8: Guidelines for Caring: My Progress
Activity Sheet 9: Guidelines for Giving the Changing the Norms Survey
Activity Sheet 10: Changing the Norms (Part 1): Survey
Activity Sheet 11: Changing the Norms (Part 2): My Plan

Display Chart 1: Mission
Display Chart 2: Agreements
Handout 5: "Be the Change" Message Cards

Optional: Wristbands that say *Be the change you wish to see in the world.* (Other options for reminders to be a positive influence are a leather cord bracelet, safety pin with beads, ribbon, friendship bracelet, or some other creative token that participants can make. You could also simply give the "Be the Change" Message Cards.)

Preparation:

- Read the lesson and think about how to facilitate it to meet your group's and school's particular needs. Keep in mind that the scripted parts (shown in italics) of the lesson provide only suggested language. Feel free to modify to fit your own style and your group's unique goals.
- Be ready to distribute each participant's completed Activity Sheets 1 and 2 (Guidelines for Caring, Parts 1 and 2) from Lesson 3.
- Make copies of Activity Sheets 8, 9, 10, and 11, one of each per participant (see pages 128–132).
- If you plan to distribute the "Be the Change" wristbands, make sure you have ordered and received them (see page 9 for ordering information). If you are going to make your own inspirational gifts, make sure you have the materials to do that.
- Make copies of Handout 5 (see page 100) on colored card stock (or laminate the cards). Cut out individual cards so they easily fit into the plastic bags containing the wristbands.
- If you choose to use the wristbands, insert one card with each wristband so that the writing is visible from the outside of the bag. (Note: This can be done prior to the meeting or can be incorporated into the lesson.)
- Display the 40 Developmental Assets, as well as Display Charts 1 and 2, where all participants can see them.

GO

Review of Previous Meetings

1 Welcome participants, thank them for being here, and **REMIND** them: *We are here today to continue with our efforts to improve our school. What is our mission?*

Refer to Display Chart 1, Mission, and **SAY** *Our mission is to promote a safer and more supportive school climate, to help build more caring relationships, and to understand the importance of the Developmental Assets.*

ASK *What did we discuss at our last meeting?* (Review.)

Explain that the purpose of ongoing meetings is to remind ourselves of the importance of continuing to make a difference in our school.

Refer to Display Chart 2, Agreements, and give a brief review.

2 **SAY** *Who remembers the definition of a norm from our earlier discussion? What is a norm?* **(A generally accepted standard of behavior.)**

ASK *Who can give me an example of a norm?* **(Driving on the right side of the road; shaking hands when you meet someone.)**

Assessing Progress for the Caring Plans

3 **ASK** for a show of hands: *Who remembers the Be the Change activity, when we completed the two Guidelines for Caring activity sheets—the Self-Inventory and the Plan? Does anyone remember the purpose of that activity?* (Take several responses.)

4 **EXPLAIN** *Today we will have an opportunity to revisit your survey of your personal norms and to check your progress with your plan. Afterward, we will also examine a strategy to encourage your friends to adopt positive norms.*

Pass out each individual's completed Activity Sheets 1 and 2, Guidelines for Caring (Part 1): Self-Inventory, and Guidelines for Caring (Part 2): The Plan.

5 **SAY** *Please review your self-inventory and then read and reflect on the progress of your plan.* Give participants about 5 minutes to read and reflect.

When time is up, distribute Activity Sheet 8. Review the activity sheet and give participants about 5 minutes to complete the following statements:

After reviewing my Guidelines for Caring, Self-Inventory and Plan, I see that:

- I am doing well promoting the positive norms by _____

- I need to improve by _____

6 When time is up, form groups of four. **EXPLAIN** *Please share your findings in your groups. Any questions?* Give participants 6 to 8 minutes to complete the task.

When time is up, **ASK** *Would any of you like to share what you learned or realized from doing this activity and from your discussion?* (Take several responses, and share any of your observations.)

Spreading the Caring Message to Friends

7 Then **ASK** *Among our peers, how do you think we can promote the positive norms of respect, consideration, and kindness toward others?* **(Modeling appropriate behavior; talking to friends.)**

8 **SAY** *We have a tool that is designed to help you help your friends to clarify their norms. It also may encourage them to join us in adopting positive norms and discouraging negativity.*

9 Distribute Activity Sheets 10 and 11. Briefly explain the survey and the plan, showing the similarities to Guidelines for Caring from Lesson 3. **SAY** *I'd like you to give this survey to your friends, one at a time.*

10 Distribute Activity Sheet 9, and **SAY** *These are the directions for giving the survey.*

11 Model (or have two participants model) giving the survey to a student. Be sure to follow the outline on Activity Sheet 9. When it is appropriate, speak your thoughts out loud to enhance understanding.

After modeling and offering any further explanation that is needed, **ASK** *Any questions?*

12 **EXPLAIN** *Find a partner, and then refer to the guidelines for using the survey. Then look over the survey and the plan activity sheets. With your partner, quickly practice giving the survey. Don't write on the survey, but just practice to get a sense of how you should give the survey. I would like one of the pair to give the survey and one to pretend to take the survey. Remember to use the guidelines! Any questions?*

Allow about 10 minutes for practice. Monitor participants' progress and provide guidance to individuals as needed.

When time is up, **ASK** *Are there any questions or comments?*

EXPLAIN *In order for this to work, we need to take this activity seriously and to remember the confidentiality rule. Give the completed survey and plan to your friend. Ask her or him to keep them and refer to them from time to time.*

13 Explain to students that when they are done with the survey, they should thank their friend and give her or him the gift and/or message card.

The message states:
Be the Change You Wish to See in the World!
Thank you for caring and taking the survey! Our mission is to help create a more caring school. Please help us by remembering and acting on your plan. Every day, you have many opportunities to truly make a difference and to be that positive force in your world. Please accept our appreciation gift as a gentle reminder for you to . . .
Be the change!

14 **EXPLAIN** *Our confidentiality rule demands that we not talk to others specifically about our friends' responses. I would like you to give me a note stating to whom you gave the survey and that person's general response to the survey. For example, your note could state, "I gave the survey to Doug. He seemed receptive and said he would try to quit teasing others and to be more open to meeting others."*

Sign your name to the note and turn it in to me. Then I will give you another copy of the survey. Our goal is for each of you to give the survey to at least three friends.

ASK *Will this process work with your friends? Why or why not?* Discuss and resolve any concerns.

15 **ASK** the group: *What did we learn from this activity and how does this relate to our mission of promoting a more caring and supportive school climate?* **(We need to spread the message; we need to be intentional about promoting the positive norms; if we all followed through on our plan, we would make a difference; if we ask friends to help promote the positive norms, that will make a difference.)**

16 Collect Activity Sheets 1 and 2, Guidelines for Caring, and file them back in participants' personal folders. Also collect Activity Sheet 8, Guidelines for Caring: My Progress, and file those in the personal folders as well. **EXPLAIN** *In future meetings, we will have a chance to review our handouts.*

Thank the group for sharing and for making a difference.

Discuss when and where the next meeting will be. If possible, establish the time and place now.

Closure

17 Close with the entire group standing in a circle, and **ASK** *Would anyone like to share anything with this group (feelings, thoughts, words of encouragement, etc.)?*

Thank the group for its commitment and willingness to help make the school a better place. Once again, state the date, time, and location of the next meeting.

MAKE A DIFFERENCE

Note: Since this lesson is long, you may want to break it up into two meetings. Consider presenting steps 1–13 and closing with steps 16–18 in one meeting. For the second meeting, after a brief review, do the role-play scenarios (step 14); continue with steps 15–18 to complete the lesson.

READY

Summary: This lesson identifies situations in which people are hurting others. Participants will have discussions and role-play situations to develop strategies to intervene. Participants are challenged to intervene early when others need help.

SET

Time Required: 90 minutes

Assets Promoted: Caring School Climate, Community Values Youth, Youth as Resources, Positive Peer Influence, Caring, Service to Others, Resistance Skills, Peaceful Conflict Resolution, Equality and Social Justice, Planning and Decision Making, Personal Power

Materials Needed:

List or poster of the 40 Developmental Assets
Display Chart 1: Mission
Display Chart 2: Agreements
Display Chart 10: Tips for Intervening

Handout 6: Emily's Story and Sonya's Story
Handouts 7–12: Role-Play Scenarios A–F

Preparation:

- Read the lesson and think about how to facilitate it to meet your group's and school's particular needs. Keep in mind that the scripted parts (shown in italics) of the lesson provide only suggested language. Feel free to modify to fit your own style and your group's unique goals.
- Select three students to role-play an unkind act (see ❸).
- Select a student, preferably male, to read Emily's Story; select another student, preferably female, to read Sonya's Story.
- Make copies of Handout 6 (see pages 101–102), one for each participant.
- Make copies of Handouts 7–12 (see pages 103–108). Cut sheets in half to create role-play cards, one Role-Play Scenario per group of four.
- Make Display Chart 10 (see page 113), using poster board or flip-chart paper. (Do not display this chart until the appropriate time during the lesson [see ⑮].)
- Display the 40 Developmental Assets, as well as Display Charts 1 and 2, where all participants can see them.

GO

Review of Previous Meetings

1 Welcome participants, thank them for being here, and REMIND them: *We are here today to continue with our efforts to improve our school. What is our mission?*

Refer to Display Chart 1, Mission, and SAY *Our mission is to promote a safer and more supportive school climate, to help build more caring relationships, and to understand the importance of the Developmental Assets.*

ASK *What did we discuss at our last meeting?* (Review.)

Explain that the purpose of ongoing meetings is to remind ourselves of the importance of continuing to make a difference in our school.

Refer to Display Chart 2, Agreements, and give a brief review.

Role-Play Activity

2 SAY *Today we are going to give you an opportunity to discuss some of the mean things that happen in school and how to help stop them.*

3 ASK *Has anyone recently seen or experienced an act of meanness at school?* (Take a few responses.)

Choose one of the experiences and set it up as a role-play scenario or have one prepared before the meeting.

4 Ask three students to role-play a mean act in which one student is taunted and teased by the others. Allow the role play to go on for 30 to 40 seconds; then freeze the scene.

5 ASK the group: *What's happening here?* (Take several responses.)

Then ASK *Is this kind of scenario a rare event in our school?* (Reach a consensus that it happens too often.) *What can we do to make a difference for the person who was being teased?* (Take several responses.)

6 Then ASK *Why even bother to help someone, especially if you don't know that person?* (Take several responses.)

The Bystander and the Hero

7 SAY *When you witness a situation like this, you have a choice—you can either be a passive bystander or you can stand up, try to stop the unkind act, and become a hero. We will now examine the roles of a bystander and a hero, as well as what it takes to be transformed from a bystander into a hero.*

8 ASK *What is a bystander?* (**One who watches and lets things happen.**)

ASK *What is a hero?* (**One who generally acts with courage and in the best interest of others.**)

9 Ask the designated (male) student to read Emily's Story.

When the story is over, ASK *What kept this student stuck in the role of a bystander? Why didn't this person act to help Emily?* (**He lacked awareness of the situation; he received little or no guidance from peers or adults in his life; he wasn't empowered, guided, or challenged to make a difference; he accepted the social norm of that group.**)

ASK *Looking back, how does this person feel about the way he acted toward Emily?* (**Guilty, ashamed, ignorant.**)

10 ASK *What could this student have done to make a positive difference in Emily's life?* (**He could have kept Emily as a friend; he could have helped convince his new friends to show more respect to Emily; he could have told others to stop being mean to her; he could have asked for help from adults in the school.**)

11 SAY *Now we are going to hear Sonya's Story, which has a different kind of ending.* Ask the designated (female) student to read Sonya's Story.

When the student finishes reading the story, ASK *Why did this student move from the role of a bystander to the role of a hero? Why did this person help Sonya?* (**She was being true to herself; she could not tolerate the mean acts anymore; she was courageous; she understood what was the right thing to do; she had empathy toward Sonya; she felt guilty for not acting; she understood she had power and was willing to use it.**)

ASK *What is empathy?* (**Compassion, sensitivity, feeling someone else's pain.**) *Did this person feel compassion for Sonya?* (**Yes.**) *Did you feel empathy for Sonya?*

ASK *How do you feel about Kevin?* (Take several responses.) *Do you know someone like Kevin? Would you or are you able to stand up against someone like Kevin?* (Take several responses.)

12 **ASK** *Do these kinds of scenarios (Emily's and Sonya's stories) happen in our school?* (Reach a consensus that it happens too often.)

Strategies to Stop Mean Acts

13 **SAY** to students: *In a moment, we are going to get into groups, and I will give a different scenario to each group. I would like each group to review the scenario and develop a strategy to stop the meanness. Then I would like each group to present a role play that illustrates your plan.*

Form participants into groups of four. Pass out a Role-Play Scenario card to each group.

Ask that the groups spread out around the room or to other rooms so that they will not overhear one another. Allow about 15 minutes for the groups to work on their assignments.

14 When time is up, or when the groups are done, ask one group at a time to present its role play.

Begin with the first role-play scenario. Be ready to record on chart paper the steps that each group went through to solve the problem.

Focus discussion on the benefits of intervening versus doing nothing.

Continue until all role-play scenarios have been performed and discussed.

15 After all groups are done role playing, show them Display Chart 10, Tips for Intervening.

Be sure to cover the following points:
- Get involved early, before the situation gets out of hand.
- Confront the *behaviors* of the individuals. Reject the behavior, not the person.
- Don't do anything that will put you in harm's way. Remember: Safety first!
- Work one-on-one. Trying to convince a large group is much more difficult.
- Ask adults for help. Find adults you trust and have a relationship with who will help you.
- Don't carry the burden by yourself. Work with this group and others in the school.

16 **ASK** *What did we learn from this activity and what does it have to do with our mission of helping to create a more caring and supportive school climate?* (**We need to discourage the negative norms and promote the positive norms; we need to be leaders and act to help others; we need to be courageous; if we stand up to people who are unkind to others, they will begin to see that their actions will not be tolerated in our school and they will stop.**)

17 Thank the group for sharing and for making a difference.

Discuss when and where the next meeting will be. If possible, establish the time and place now.

Closure

18 Close with the group standing in a circle, and **ASK** *Would anyone like to share anything with this group (feelings, thoughts, words of encouragement, etc.)?*

Thank the group for its commitment and willingness to help make the school a better place. Once again, state the date, time, and location of the next meeting.

THE PERSON WHO CARED

READY

Summary: This lesson provides an opportunity for participants to recognize and thank those in the school who have supported them. Students identify and write thank-you cards to supportive adults. Adults identify and write thank-you cards to supportive students.

SET

Time Required: 30 minutes

Assets Promoted: Other Adult Relationships, Caring School Climate, Youth as Resources, Service to Others, Adult Role Models, High Expectations, Positive Peer Influence, Caring, Honesty, Responsibility, Interpersonal Competence

Materials Needed:

List or poster of the 40 Developmental Assets
Flip-chart paper on a stand with markers
Poster board or flip-chart paper
Blank thank-you cards and envelopes, one set per participant

Display Chart 1: Mission
Display Chart 2: Agreements
Display Chart 11: Thank You!

Preparation:

- Read the lesson and think about how to facilitate it to meet your group's and school's particular needs. Keep in mind that the scripted parts (shown in italics) of the lesson provide only suggested language. Feel free to modify to fit your own style and your group's unique goals.
- Have thank-you cards/envelopes ready to distribute.
- Prepare to tell the group about an important adult from your secondary school years (see **2**).
- Make Display Chart 11 (see page 114), using poster board or flip-chart paper. (Do not display this chart until the appropriate time during the lesson [see **8**].)
- Display the 40 Developmental Assets, as well as Display Charts 1 and 2, where all participants can see them.

GO

Review of Previous Meetings

1 Welcome participants, thank them for being here, and REMIND them: *We are here today to continue with our efforts to improve our school. What is our mission?*

Refer to Display Chart 1, Mission, and

SAY *Our mission is to promote a safer and more supportive school climate, to help build more caring relationships, and to understand the importance of the Developmental Assets.*

ASK *What did we discuss at our last meeting?* (Review.)

Explain that the purpose of ongoing meetings is to remind ourselves of the importance of continuing to make a difference in our school.

Refer to Display Chart 2, Agreements, and give a brief review.

Who Supports You?

2 **SAY** *Today our focus is to improve relationships between adults and students in our school.*

Tell the group about an important adult in your school life (when you were an adolescent). Explain the specifics about that person and the nature of the support he or she gave you. Describe the long-term benefits to you of this person's support.

3 **ASK** these questions (without pausing for responses between each one):
- *Who is or has been an important adult from your school life?*
- *Who has been there to support you?*
- *Who has had a positive impact in your life?*
- *Who has encouraged you, has made learning fun, or has been an asset builder in your life?*

Then **SAY** *Remember, to accomplish this mission, our focus must be on the adults in this school.* (Ask the adults in the room to talk about the adults who were important in their lives when they were teenagers.)

4 **ASK** participants to find a partner, and give them the following instructions:

I would like you to discuss with your partner a person who is making or has made a difference in your life. Tell your partner what the person did to have a positive impact on you. It could be something the person did or said, or the way the person treated you. You will have about 3 minutes each to share your story. Any questions?

5 When time is up, ask for a few volunteers to share their stories of the adult who had a positive impact on them.

6 Focus on some of the ways that adults made a positive impact on young people:
- Supporting them no matter what they did;
- Valuing what they said or did;
- Setting high expectations for them;

- Doing fun things with them;
- Listening to them;
- Getting them interested in school;
- Teaching them positive values such as honesty and responsibility;
- Helping them get along with others;
- Sharing their life experience with them;
- Giving them a positive view of their personal future.

Giving Thanks

7 Hand out the thank-you cards and envelopes (one set per person). **SAY** *Now we are going to write a thank-you note to the adults in the school who have made a difference for us. Try to think of an adult who works in this school, but if you can't, write to any adult (other than your own parents) who has made a difference in your life.*

Tell the adults to write a thank-you note to a student in the school. **SAY** *You could write to a student who has supported you, is cooperative, is an eager learner, is helpful, or is just fun to be around.*

8 Refer to Display Chart 11, Thank You!, and tell participants that you would like them to do at least three things in their card:
- Describe what the person specifically did to have a positive impact on you;
- Thank the person for having done that;
- Encourage the person to do the same for others.

9 Tell participants to place their card in the envelope without sealing it when they are done. Then they can address the envelope with the person's name. Explain that they can deliver the cards later or that you can collect the cards and deliver them after the meeting. (Find a volunteer to handle this task. Do not distribute any cards during the meeting.)

ASK *Any questions?*

10 When time is up, **ASK** *Would any of you like to read your card to the group?* (Take several volunteers, applauding after each card is read.)

Next, have students seal the envelopes. Then collect the cards that are to be distributed by the volunteer.

ASK *How did it feel to write your thank-you card?* (Take several responses.)

ASK the group: *What's the point of this activity and how does it apply to our mission?* **(It is good to thank those who have supported us; thanking people encourages them to continue to be supportive of others; it strengthens the relationship.)**

Explain to the group that cards are inexpensive. **SAY** *This is a simple but powerful activity. I encourage all of you to write an occasional thank-you note to people who have supported you.* (You may even consider having a supply of cards and envelopes available to students.) *It is good to acknowledge those who encourage us. Remember the saying, "What goes around comes around!" Those who receive cards are more likely to continue to encourage and support others, benefiting us all.*

11 Thank the group for sharing and for making a difference.

Discuss when and where the next meeting will be. If possible, establish the time and place now.

Closure

12 Close with the group standing in a circle, and **ASK** *Would anyone like to share anything with this group (feelings, thoughts, words of encouragement, etc.)?*

Thank the group for its commitment and willingness to help make the school a better place. Once again, state the date, time, and location of the next meeting.

UNDER MY WING

Note: Make sure you have presented Lesson 15 before doing this one.

READY

Summary: Participants have an opportunity to recognize their power to influence younger people in a positive way. Participants identify a younger person and create a plan to build a stronger, more positive relationship with that person.

SET

Time Required: 30 minutes

Assets Promoted: Caring School Climate, Community Values Youth, Youth as Resources, Service to Others, High Expectations, Positive Peer Influence, Caring, Honesty, Responsibility, Interpersonal Competence, Personal Power

Materials Needed:

List or poster of the 40 Developmental Assets
Display Chart 1: Mission
Display Chart 2: Agreements

Activity Sheet 12: Under My Wing
Blank 3"x 3" sticky notes, three per person

Preparation:

- Read the lesson and think about how to facilitate it to meet your group's and school's particular needs. Keep in mind that the scripted parts (shown in italics) of the lesson provide only suggested language. Feel free to modify to fit your own style and your group's unique goals.
- Prepare to give an example of what you are intentionally doing to make a positive difference in a young person's life (see ❸).
- Have the sticky notes ready to distribute.
- Make copies of Activity Sheet 12 (see page 133), one per participant.
- Display the 40 Developmental Assets, as well as Display Charts 1 and 2, where all participants can see them.

GO

Review of Previous Meetings

❶ Welcome participants, thank them for being here, and **REMIND** them: *We are here today to continue with our efforts to improve our school. What is our mission?*

Refer to Display Chart 1, Mission, and

SAY *Our mission is to promote a safer and more supportive school climate, to help build more caring relationships, and to understand the importance of the Developmental Assets.*

ASK *What did we discuss at our last meeting?* (Review.)

Explain that the purpose of ongoing meetings is to remind ourselves of the importance of continuing to make a difference in our school.

Refer to Display Chart 2, Agreements, and give a brief review.

Make a Difference for Someone Else

2 **SAY** *The last time we met, you each identified an adult in the school who is making a difference in your life. You wrote a thank-you note to that person. I want you to know that you also have the power to make a difference in others' lives.*

Today, you will have an opportunity to use your "power of one" to intentionally become a positive influence in a younger person's life. What does "intentional" mean? **(To thoughtfully and carefully plan to do something, or, as we commonly say, to do it on purpose.)**

SAY *Today, I'd like you to identify one younger person and think about how you intentionally make a positive difference in her or his life.*

3 Give an example of a younger person in whose life you are intentionally making a positive difference. Tell the group some of things you do with and for this person to build her or his assets.

4 **SAY** *I would like you to think about one younger person in whose life you make a positive difference. This person may be a younger brother or sister, cousin, niece, or nephew. This person could be a friend's younger brother or sister. This person could live in your neighborhood, ride your bus, or be someone you see fairly often.*

5 **EXPLAIN** *Turn to a partner and briefly share a few things about the younger person you thought of: Who the person is, what you are doing now to make a positive difference in that person's life, and/or what you could do to make more of a positive difference in that person's life. Any questions?* Give participants about 3 minutes for this activity.

6 When they are finished, ask several volunteers to share what they discussed. Thank and applaud those who share what they have done or plan to do.

SAY *Think about the adults you wrote thank-you notes to at the last meeting. Think about the things that person has done for you, how he or she treats you, and how special that makes you feel. That's a great example of how you can show younger people that you care about them.*

Small Group Activity

7 **EXPLAIN** *I would like you to form into groups of three or four. Group with people you know fairly well and will see during the coming week.*

8 Distribute three sticky notes to each participant and **GIVE** the following instructions:

On each of the three sticky notes you have, please write what you said you would do to make a difference for the young person. Write the same thing on each sticky note.

At the beginning of every day, I would like you to think about what you're going to do for the young person. So when you get home today, place the first note where you will see it in the first five minutes of each day, for example, on your alarm clock or your bathroom mirror. When you see the note in the morning, visualize doing the activity during the day.

Place the second note where you'll see it in the middle of the day, for example, in your lunchbox, at your desk, or in your locker.

Place the third note where you'll see it in the evening. The idea is for you to be continually reminded about how you're going to have a positive impact on the young person you care about.

When everyone in your group has written the three notes, share what you've written with the rest of your group. Give the groups about 5 minutes to talk about what they have written.

Sharing and Asking for Support

9 **SAY** *I'm sure you've all heard the phrase "under my wing." What is the meaning of that phrase?* **(Adult birds shelter and protect their young, especially in the nest, under their wings.)**
SAY *In a sense, you will be doing the same for a younger person!*

Distribute Activity Sheet 12, briefly explain it, and allow about 5 minutes for participants to complete the handout.

(10) When time is up, ask participants to share in their group. Ask that each participant find one person to sign her or his sheet as a witness.

Then **SAY** *The person who signs as a witness will support you in accomplishing what you said you are going to do. It could be as simple as to ask you whether you did what you said you'd do. Any questions?*

Give participants about 3 minutes to complete this activity.

(11) When time is up, allow several volunteers to share with the larger group what they have written. After each person has spoken, be sure to **ASK** *Who is your witness?*

(12) **ASK** *What's the point of this activity and how does it apply to our mission of promoting a more caring and supportive school climate?* (**When we support others, we build their assets and our own; by intentionally making a difference for a younger person, we enrich her or his life and our own; helping younger students will help our school and community now and in the future.**)

(13) **SAY** *It is important to be aware of the power we have and to use it in a positive way. We can make a difference in a younger person's life and leave a legacy of support and care that can continue in our school even after we are gone.*

(14) Collect the activity sheets. Explain that you will file the sheets in the students' personal folders, and they can review them at future meetings. Then **REMIND** participants:

Be sure to place your sticky notes where you will see them three times a day.

Thank the group for sharing and for making a difference.

Discuss when and where the next meeting will be. If possible, establish the time and place now.

Closure

(15) Close with the entire group standing in a circle, and **ASK** *Would anyone like to share anything with this group (feelings, thoughts, words of encouragement, etc.)?*

Thank the group for its commitment and willingness to help make the school a better place. Once again, state the date, time, and location of the next meeting.

LET'S CONNECT! PART 1

Note: This is the first of a two-part lesson (Lessons 17 and 18). In this lesson, you will teach three activities to the group. Participants will then prepare to teach the same activities to a larger group of students and staff from the general school population on another day (Lesson 18/Part 2).

READY

Summary: This lesson provides an opportunity for participants to learn three enjoyable connecting activities that will be presented to a larger group of students at another time. Participants will also select and prepare to present one of the activities to the larger group of students.

SET

Time Required: 45 minutes

Assets Promoted: Caring School Climate, Youth as Resources, Service to Others, High Expectations, Positive Peer Influence, Bonding to School, Caring, Honesty, Responsibility, Interpersonal Competence, Sense of Purpose

Materials Needed:

List or poster of the 40 Developmental Assets
Display Chart 1: Mission
Display Chart 2: Agreements
Description of Lesson 18: Let's Connect! (Part 2)

Beach ball
Blank 3"x 5" index cards, one per participant
Activity Sheet 13: Invitation
Pens and pencils

Preparation:

- Read the lesson and think about how to facilitate it to meet your group's and school's particular needs. Keep in mind that the scripted parts (shown in italics) of the lesson provide only suggested language. Feel free to modify to fit your own style and your group's unique goals.
- Make copies of Lesson 18 (see pages 70–74) for those who volunteer to present parts of that lesson to the larger group. (You should have two to four student presenters for each of the five activities.)
- Display the 40 Developmental Assets, as well as Display Charts 1 and 2, where all participants can see them.
- Make copies of Activity Sheet 13 (see page 134), several per participant.

GO

Review of Previous Meetings

1 Welcome participants, thank them for being here, and **REMIND** them: *We are here today to continue with our efforts to improve our school. What is our mission?*

Refer to Display Chart 1, Mission, and

SAY *Our mission is to promote a safer and more supportive school climate, to help build more caring relationships, and to feel the power of the Developmental Assets.*

ASK *What did we discuss at our last meeting?* (Review.)

Explain that the purpose of ongoing meetings is to remind ourselves of the importance of continuing to make a difference in our school.

Refer to Display Chart 2, Agreements, and give a brief review.

2 **EXPLAIN** *Today we are going to participate in three activities that we will present to a larger group of about 40 students in our school. The purpose of these activities is to have fun, to get to know each other better, and to give all of us an opportunity to make some connections with others that we might not otherwise make.*

After we learn these activities, I will ask for volunteers to present each activity at the meeting with the larger group. So, as we participate in these activities, I want you to think about whether this is an activity that you would like to present.

Explain to the participants when and where you anticipate presenting the activities to the larger group.

3 **SAY** *The three activities are called, Do You Know Your Neighbors?, Getting Carded, and 100 Times! In a moment, we are going to experience each of those activities in an abbreviated form. After we review the activities, we will discuss how we will present these activities to the larger group at a later time.*

The First Activity

4 **EXPLAIN** *Let's get seated in a circle of chairs. You should have nothing in your hands, nothing by your feet, and, for safety purposes, no pens or pencils in your pockets, behind your ears, etc. The first activity is called Do You Know Your Neighbors?*

Stand in the center of the circle and **SAY** *I will begin by standing in the middle of the circle. Then I will introduce myself by my first name (if an adult, by last name). Everyone will respond by saying Hi and my name.* (Give an example using your name.)

SAY *I will then call on someone and say (for example), "Stan, do you know your neighbors?" Stan will introduce his neighbor on his one side, then introduce his neighbor on the other side. For*

instance, he will say, "Yes, this is my neighbor Amanda, and this is my neighbor Kimberly."

After Stan is done introducing his neighbors, he says that he would like to get to know everyone in the circle who has a particular thing in common with him. For instance, he could say, "I would like to get to know everyone who has ever been on an airplane." (Other examples could be asking for people whose favorite color is blue, have a best friend, or are fans of a certain sports team, etc.) Stan should say something that he probably has in common with lots of people in the circle.

Next, everyone who has, for instance, been on an airplane, has to stand up and quickly find another seat. Stan, too, will stand up and find a new chair. You cannot move to the chair next to you. You need to find a seat at least five chairs away. I will sit down, too, so the last person standing will stand in the center of the circle and do as I did. That person will first introduce her- or himself, then ask someone seated the question, "Do you know your neighbors?" Any questions so far?

5 **EXPLAIN** *Remember our agreement of safety. There is to be no sprinting; we need to walk quickly but safely.*

Demonstrate a safety issue by asking a volunteer to stand up in the circle with you. **SAY** *If you and another person see the same chair at the same time, rather than run and jump into it (and possibly hurting someone), the first person to get a hand on the chair, claims that chair, so there is no need to jump or dive into a chair.* (Model with the volunteer.)

SAY *Finally, after you are seated in a new chair by different people, you will need to introduce yourself to your new neighbors. Introduce yourself just to your neighbors on either side of you. Any questions?* Answer any questions, and then begin the game. Play about 10 rounds so that all have a chance to get a good sense of the activity.

When finished, **ASK** *What are your thoughts about this activity? Do you think a larger group of students would enjoy it?* Facilitate a brief discussion. Then **SAY** *When we present this to the larger group we will ask them, "What's the point of this activity and what does it have to do with our mission?"* (**To get to know each other's names; to show how much we have in common; to break the ice and feel more comfortable with each other.**)

The Second Activity

6 Introduce the next activity, Getting Carded. (This activity may already have been presented as it is part of Lesson 8, Getting to Know You. If it has been presented, briefly review the activity and skip to #11.)

SAY *Please open the circle so we are now in a semicircle with the opening toward the front and the flip-chart stand (or board).*

7 Pass out an index card to each person. Be sure everyone has a pen or pencil.

Tell participants that they will be putting a great deal of information on this card, so they should not make their letters too large. Also, have them orient their card horizontally (landscape), not vertically (portrait).

SAY *You will share what you write on these cards with the group, so don't write anything you wouldn't be comfortable sharing.*

Ask them to write the following on their index cards. (Do not prepare the chart in advance. As you tell them what to write on their cards, write an example of each item on chart paper or an erasable board.)

- *In the center of the card, write #1 and your name.*
- *In the upper left-hand corner of the card, write #2 and your favorite sport.*
- *In the upper right-hand corner of the card, write #3 and your favorite place to be (inside or outside).*
- *In the lower left-hand corner of the card, write #4 and the name of someone significant in your life (parent, grandparent, aunt, uncle, sibling, etc.).*
- *In the lower right-hand corner of the card, write #5 and something positive about yourself (friendly, dependable, etc.).*
- *Below your name, write #6 and the name of a famous person in history who you admire (you don't need to write out why, but be prepared to talk about that).*
- *On the back of the card near the top, write #7 and something you are proud of (an accomplishment, a kind deed, hard work, etc.).*
- *Under #7, write #8 and an important goal you have in your life.*
- *Under #8, write #9 and the name of someone who looks up to you as a role model.*

ASK *Any questions?*

8 When everyone has finished writing, demonstrate the remainder of the activity, first by choosing a partner. With your partner, **EXPLAIN** to the group: *I will share all nine categories that I have written on my card with my partner. My partner will listen carefully and may ask questions about anything that isn't clear.*

When I am done, my partner will share her or his card with me. I will listen attentively and try to remember as much as possible. I, too, may ask questions for clarification.

When we are done, we stay together and find another pair. This time I introduce my partner to the other pair from memory. I can use my card to help cue me, but I should not look at my partner's card. If I can't remember a point, my partner will help me. Then my partner will introduce me and, finally, the other pair will do the same. When we are all done, the partners stay together and search out a different pair and repeat the process.

ASK *Any questions?*

9 Ask participants to stand up and find someone they don't know very well to be their partner. Recommend that adults pair with students. After everyone has a partner, tell the group members they have about 8 minutes to do all the introductions and then have them begin.

10 After about 8 minutes, ask participants to return to their seats, sitting by their partner, in the semicircle.

Ask the group if any of them would like to share what they learned that was particularly interesting about others in this room. (Take several responses.)

11 When finished, **ASK** *What are your thoughts about Getting Carded? Do you think a larger group of students would enjoy it?* Facilitate a brief discussion. Then **SAY** *When we present this to the larger group we will ask them, "What is the point of this activity and what does it have to do with our mission statement?"* **(Get to know each other better; find out new things about people; talk to people you may not normally talk to.)**

The Third Activity

(12) **SAY** *Finally, our last activity is called 100 Times and for this activity we will all need to sit on the floor.* (Allow the option for adults or others with physical limitations to sit in chairs and still participate.) (This activity may already have been presented, as it is part of Lesson 1, Mission *Is* Possible. If it has been presented, briefly review the activity and skip to #13.)

EXPLAIN *We will need to all sit together and fill up the floor space so that there are no large gaps between people. For safety purposes, make sure you are sitting down all the way, and not up on your knees.*

ASK with beach ball in hand: *Who knows what a metaphor is?* **(A figure of speech comparing two unrelated objects or ideas.)** *Can you give me an example of a metaphor?* **("The world's a stage;" "You are my sunshine.")** *This beach ball is a metaphor for kindness. Your task is to tap the beach ball 25 times without its touching the ground. If it touches the ground, we will start over again. Also, the 25 times is an abbreviated number, as our goal for the larger group will be at least 100 times.*

EXPLAIN the rules: *The ball represents the kind acts we will all offer. We need to pass the ball (the kindness) around our circle here, the way we will pass acts of kindness around the school. You cannot tap the ball two consecutive times, and you can't pass the ball between just two or three people. Also, we all need to count together in unison.*

Toss the beach ball into the air over the group and have everyone count the taps aloud. If the ball touches the ground, start over.

Each time the ball falls to the ground, **ASK** the group: *What do we need to do to make this work?* Do this several times, until the group completes the task.

(13) When finished, **ASK** *What are your thoughts about this activity? Do you think a larger group of students would enjoy it?* Allow time for discussion. Then **SAY** *When we present this to the larger group we will ask them, "What is the point of this activity and what does it have to do with our mission statement?"* **(Little things count; individuals are important and everyone can make a difference; if we band together we can be more successful, and changing the school climate will also depend on how well we work together;**

we need to keep our eye on the ball or keep the mission in mind.)

Planning to Present

(14) **SAY** *Now we have to look at how we are to present these activities to a larger group of students. We also want to take advantage of our time with this group to weave in a message about our mission—to create a more caring school and to invite them to join us in our efforts.*

EXPLAIN *There are basically five parts to present to the large group. They are the three activities we just reviewed plus an introduction and a closure. I have a description and suggested script for Lesson 18 that I will give to each volunteer, so you can practice your part. We need at least two people leading each activity.*

(15) Give an overview of all five parts (Introduction, Do You Know Your Neighbors?, Getting Carded, 100 Times, and Closure) with more explanation for the Introduction and the Closure.

Ask for pairs or teams of volunteers to present each of the five parts.

(16) Distribute the copies of Lesson 18 to the teams. Allow time for participants to read and to prepare their parts. Answer any questions that they may have. Determine the date, time, and location (large open room) for the session. Make sure to allow at least 60 minutes for the session.

(17) Discuss who could or should participate. Should it be by personal invitation, class invitation, open invitation, etc.? Also discuss the number of students (ideally, 25–35) and staff (ideally, 2–3) to invite to the session.

Distribute Activity Sheet 13, Invitation.
SAY *In this invitation, we emphasize that we need the people we invite to participate fully in the activities. We will participate fully as well. In fact, those who are not presenting should mix it up with the larger group of participants and be models for enthusiasm and full participation. If you are presenting, you should be well prepared. When you present, please don't read your part. The activities are good, but the delivery of the activity is critical. Please study, practice, and know your parts. If you have any questions or concerns, please see me. Any questions or comments?*

Then **SAY** *Finally, if you are not presenting, we would like you to participate fully, too! Also, during our discussions after the activities, please speak up about your thoughts and ideas on the importance of helping to create a more caring school and building better relationships between and among everyone.*

18 Thank the group for sharing and for making a difference. Remind them again when and where the next meeting will be.

Closure

19 Close with the entire group standing in a circle, **ASK** *Would anyone like to share anything with this group (feelings, thoughts, words of encouragement, etc.)?*

Thank the group for its commitment and willingness to help make the school a better place. Once again, state the date, time, and location of the next meeting.

LET'S CONNECT! PART 2

Note: This is the second of a two-part lesson. In this lesson, the students facilitate activities with a larger group. In Part 1(Lesson 17), the students prepared to present the activities listed below.

READY

Summary: This lesson gives students and staff an opportunity to connect with each other in a fun and playful way. A small team of students will facilitate the activities of the large group.

SET

Time Required: 60 minutes

Assets Promoted: Caring School Climate, Youth as Resources, Service to Others, High Expectations, Positive Peer Influence, Bonding to School, Caring, Honesty, Responsibility, Interpersonal Competence, Sense of Purpose, Safety

Materials Needed:

List or poster of the 40 Developmental Assets
Display Chart 1: Mission
Display Chart 2: Agreements
Display Chart 4: Quote from Aesop
Display Chart 5: Quote from Gandhi

Display Chart 6: Quote from Margaret Mead
Flip-chart paper and stand
Blank 3"x 5" index cards, one per participant
Pencils
Beach ball

Optional: Wristbands that say *No act of kindness, no matter how small, is ever wasted,* one per participant. (Other options for kindness recognition items are a leather cord bracelet, safety pin with beads, ribbon, friendship bracelet, or some other creative token that participants can make before presenting this lesson.)
Optional: Handout 4: Kindness Recognition Cards, one per participant.

Preparation:

• Set up a large room with 50+ chairs arranged in a semicircle facing the flip-chart stand.

• Display the 40 Developmental Assets, as well as Display Charts 1, 2, 4, 5, and 6, around the room.

• Students who are presenting should practice their presentations before the meeting. Think about how to facilitate the games to meet your group's and school's particular needs. Keep in mind that the scripted parts (shown in italics) provide only suggested language. Feel free to modify to fit your own style and your group's unique goals.

• Make sure you have your chosen recognition items (e.g., wristbands, ribbons, bracelets, etc.) ready to distribute.

• If you plan to distribute Handout 4, make copies on colored card stock or laminated paper.

GO

Introduction

1 Welcome participants to the session. Introduce yourself and your co-leaders. **SAY** *We are here today to have some fun and to get to know each other better.*

Refer to Display Chart 1, Mission, and **SAY** *Our group has been working to help make our school a better place. A large part of our group's mission is to promote a safer and more supportive school climate (the feeling in the school) and to build more caring relationships among everyone in the school.* If it is appropriate, give an example of some of the things the group has done.

EXPLAIN *That is why we've invited you here as well! To help create a better feeling in the school and to build better relationships between us all! We want you to join us in making ours a more kind and respectful school.*

2 **SAY** *Do you remember our request on your invitation? For this event to be successful, we are asking each and every one of you to have a positive attitude and a playful spirit, and to participate fully in the activities. So let's forget about the stresses of the day for a little while, and just HAVE FUN!*

In a few minutes we are going to start with a getting-acquainted game. In order for us to feel safe, supported, and respected, we need to come to some agreements.

3 Refer to Display Chart 2, Agreements, and point out: *The first agreement is safety. We all want and need to be safe.*

ASK the following:
Besides physically, how else can you hurt someone? **(You can hurt someone emotionally, or, as we commonly say, you can hurt someone's feelings.)**
How can you hurt someone's feelings here today? **(By teasing or criticizing her or him.)**
How else can you hurt someone's feelings here today? **(By ignoring her or him.)**
How else can you hurt someone's feelings here today? **(By gossiping about her or him.)**
How else can you hurt someone's feelings here today? **(By excluding her or him.)**

SAY *We need to be safe here. Can we agree not to hurt anyone, either physically or emotionally?*

Continue to the next word on Display Chart 2: *The second agreement is support. We all need to feel supported. How can we support people here?* **(By offering verbal encouragement; listening to others.)**

SAY *We all need to feel supported. Can we agree to support people here today?*

Next, discuss the third word on Display Chart 2: *The last agreement is respect. How can we show respect to people here?* **(By listening to people; allowing one person to talk at a time; maintaining confidentiality so that what is said here stays here.)**

SAY *We need to be respectful of each other. Can we agree to show respect to everyone here?*

Will you follow the agreements? Show me a "thumbs-up" if you will follow the agreements. Thank you!

EXPLAIN *If anyone (including me) breaks any of the agreements, please remind her or him of that fact so we can change our behavior.*

Any questions? Thanks, and let's begin our first activity!

(Hand off to the team that will be presenting Do You Know Your Neighbors?)

NEXT PRESENTERS

4 The team presenting Do You Know Your Neighbors? should now come to the front. Introduce yourself and your co-leaders.

SAY *Our first activity is called Do You Know Your Neighbors?*

5 **EXPLAIN** *Let's begin by closing in the semicircle to form a circle of chairs. You should have nothing in your hands, nothing by your feet, and, for safety purposes, no pens or pencils in your pockets, behind your ears, etc.*

Stand in the center of the circle, and **SAY** *I will begin by standing in the middle of the circle. Then I will introduce myself by my first name (if an adult, by last name). Everyone will respond by saying Hi and my name.* (Give an example using your name.)

SAY *I will then call on someone and say (for example), "Stan, do you know your neighbors?" Stan will introduce his neighbor on his one side, then introduce his neighbor on the other side. For instance, he will say, "Yes, this is my neighbor Amanda, and this is my neighbor Kimberly."*

After Stan is done introducing his neighbors, he says that he would like to get to know everyone in the circle who has a particular thing in common with him. For instance, he could say, "I would like to get to know everyone who has ever been on an airplane." (Other examples could be asking for people whose favorite color is blue, have a best friend, or are fans of a certain sports team, etc.) Stan should say something that he probably has in common with lots of people in the circle.

Next, everyone who has, for instance, been on an airplane, has to stand up and quickly find another seat. Stan, too, will stand up and find a new chair. You cannot move to the chair next to you. You need to find a seat at least five chairs away. I will sit down too, so the last person standing will stand in the center of the circle and do as I did. That person will first introduce her- or himself, then ask someone seated the question, "Do you know your neighbors?" Any questions so far?

Before we get started, I'd like to give you all a moment to meet the people sitting next to you. If you don't know the two people sitting on either side of you, please meet them briefly now and exchange names. Every time we find a new chair, throughout the game, we introduce ourselves to our new neighbors.

6 **EXPLAIN** *Remember our agreement of safety. There is to be no sprinting; we need to walk quickly but safely.*

Demonstrate a safety issue by asking a volunteer to stand up in the circle with you. **SAY** *If you and another person see the same chair at the same time, rather than run and jump into it (and possibly hurting someone), the first person to get a hand on the chair, claims that chair, so there is no need to jump or dive into a chair.* (Model with the volunteer.)

ASK *Any questions?* Answer any questions, and then begin the game. Play about 15 rounds. When done, **ASK** the question: *What's the point of this activity and what does it have to do with our mission?* **(To get to know each other's names; to show how much we have in common; to break the ice and feel more comfortable with each other.)**

SAY *Thank you! It's time for our next activity!*

(Hand off to the team that will be presenting Getting Carded.)

NEXT PRESENTERS

7 The team presenting Getting Carded should now address the group. Introduce yourself and your co-leaders. **SAY** *The next activity is called Getting Carded.*

EXPLAIN *If we are going to make a difference in our school, it has to begin with this group of people right here. If we are going to be successful in promoting a more caring and supportive school climate we have to be caring and supportive of each other. When we have an opportunity to get to know someone better we tend to care more about that person. So today we are going to get to know each other better!*

SAY *Please open the circle so we are now in a semicircle with the opening toward the front and the flip-chart stand (or board).*

8 Pass out a 3"x 5" index card to each person. Be sure everyone has a pen or pencil.

Tell participants that they will be putting a great deal of information on this card, so they should not make their letters too large. Also, have them orient their card horizontally (landscape), not vertically (portrait).

SAY *You will share what you write on these cards with the group, so don't write anything you wouldn't be comfortable sharing.*

Ask them to write the following on their index cards. (Do not prepare the chart in advance. As you tell them what to write on their cards, write an example of each item on chart paper or erasable board.)

- *In the center of the card, write #1 and your name.*
- *In the upper left-hand corner of the card, write #2 and your favorite sport.*
- *In the upper right-hand corner of the card, write #3 and your favorite place to be (inside or outside).*
- *In the lower left-hand corner of the card, write #4 and the name of someone significant in your life (parent, grandparent, aunt, uncle, sibling, etc.).*
- *In the lower right-hand corner of the card, write #5 and something positive about yourself (friendly, dependable, etc.).*

- *Below your name, write #6 and the name of a famous person in history who you admire (you don't need to write out why, but be prepared to talk about that).*
- *On the back of the card near the top, write #7 and something you are proud of (an accomplishment, a kind deed, hard work, etc.).*
- *Under #7, write #8 and an important goal you have in your life.*
- *Under #8, write #9 and the name of someone who looks up to you as a role model.*

ASK *Any questions?*

9 When everyone has finished writing, demonstrate the remainder of the activity, first by choosing a partner. With your partner, **EXPLAIN** to the group: *I will share all nine categories that I have written on my card with my partner. My partner will listen carefully and may ask questions about anything that isn't clear.*

When I am done, my partner will share her or his card with me. I will listen attentively and try to remember as much as possible. I, too, may ask questions for clarification. When we are done, we stay together and find another pair. This time I introduce my partner to the other pair from memory. I can use my card to help cue me, but I should not look at my partner's card. If I can't remember a point, my partner will help me. Then my partner will introduce me and, finally, the other pair will do the same. When we are all done, the partners stay together and search out a different pair and repeat the process.

ASK *Any questions?*

10 Ask participants to stand up and find someone they don't know very well to be their partner. Recommend that adults pair with students. After everyone has a partner, tell the group members they have about 8 minutes to do all the introductions and then have them begin.

11 After about 8 minutes, ask participants to return to their seats in the semicircle, sitting next to their partner.

Ask the group if any of them would like to share what they learned that was particularly interesting about others in this room. (Take several responses.)

ASK *What is the point of this activity and what does it have to do with our mission statement?*

(Get to know each other better; find out new things about people; talk to people you may not normally talk to; encourage inclusion rather than exclusion.)

12 **SAY** *Thank you for your participation! It is now time for our next activity!*

(Hand off to the team that will be presenting 100 Times!)

NEXT PRESENTERS

13 The team presenting 100 Times! should now come to the front of the group. Introduce yourself and your co-leaders.

14 **SAY** *Our next activity is called 100 Times!*

Share a story of a kind act. Then read Chart 4: *No act of kindness, no matter how small, is ever wasted.* **ASK** *Can we ever waste kindness?* (Gather a consensus of no.) **ASK** *Has anyone heard the phrase "What goes around, comes around?" What does this mean?* **(If you are kind to others, that kindness spreads around and, eventually, comes back to you; if you are mean to people, that, too, can spread.)**

SAY *Our challenge to you is to be kind every day! Imagine if each of us offered three simple kind acts toward others every day, what an impact we could have in our school!*

15 **SAY** *For our last activity we will need everyone to sit on the floor.* (Allow the option for adults or others with physical limitations to sit in chairs and still participate.)

EXPLAIN *We will need to all sit together and fill up the floor space so that there are no large gaps between people. For safety purposes, make sure you are sitting down all the way, and not up on your knees.*

ASK with beach ball in hand: *Who knows what a metaphor is?* **(A figure of speech comparing two unrelated objects or ideas.)** *Can you give me an example of a metaphor?* **("The world's a stage;" "You are my sunshine.")** *This beach ball is a metaphor for kindness. Your task is to tap the beach ball 100 times without its touching the ground. If it touches the ground, we will start over.* (The number of taps can be the number of participants multiplied by three, as in the number of kind acts. This number can be as high as 200, if time allows.)

EXPLAIN the rules: *The ball represents the kind acts we will all offer. We need to pass the ball (the kindness) around our circle here, the way we will pass acts of kindness around the school. You cannot tap the ball two consecutive times, and you can't pass the ball between just two or three people. Also, we all need to count together in unison.*

Toss the beach ball into the air over the group and have everyone count the taps aloud. If the ball touches the ground, start over.

Each time the ball falls to the ground, **ASK** the group: *What do we need to do to make this work?* Do this several times, until the group completes the task.

16 When finished, **ASK** *What is the point of this activity and what does it have to do with our mission of creating a more caring school?* **(Little things count; individuals are important and everyone can make a difference; if we band together we can be more successful, and changing the school climate will also depend on how well we work together; we need to keep our eye on the ball or keep the mission in mind.)**

SAY *Thank you for participating! Now we'd like to share a few closing thoughts.*

(Hand off to the team that will be presenting the Closure.)

NEXT PRESENTERS

Closure

17 The team presenting the closure should now come to the front of the room. Introduce yourself and your co-leaders.

ASK *Do you really think we can be kinder and that each of us can truly make a difference in our school?*

ASK *How many here are willing to try? Raise your hand if you are willing to try.*

18 Refer to Display Chart 4 and **SAY** *I'd like to remind you of this quote, "No act of kindness, no matter how small, is ever wasted."* Say: *We have a gift for you. This gift will act as a reminder to be kind and to make a difference.* Show the gift your group has chosen to give.

SAY *I would like to give you one, but only if you are willing to make a commitment to make a difference, to be part of our effort, our mission, and to offer at least three acts of kindness toward others every day.*

EXPLAIN *I would also like you to wear (or display) it each day and to acknowledge those in our group when you see them. When you see each other in the halls, point to your (item) and ask, "Have you done your three acts of kindness today?"*

While everyone remains seated in the group on the floor, pass out the gifts, one for each participant.

19 Thank the group for its participation and enthusiasm.

Share any of your own thoughts about this group, acknowledging their willingness to participate, to hear the message, and to take a risk by being here today.

Also refer to the quotes by Aesop (again), Mahatma Gandhi, and Margaret Mead that are posted on the walls.

If time permits, ask if anyone else would like to share something in closing. (Take several comments.)

Thank the participants again and dismiss them.

A MORE PERFECT SCHOOL

Note: This is the first part of a two-part lesson.

READY

Summary: This lesson gives participants the opportunity to brainstorm ideas to improve their school. Participants generate ideas under the three broad categories of *Student to Student*, *Student to Adult*, and *Physical Environment*.

SET

Time Required: 45 minutes

Assets Promoted: Caring School Climate, Community Values Youth, Youth as Resources, Positive Peer Influence, Caring, Planning and Decision Making

Materials Needed:

List or poster of the 40 Developmental Assets
Display Chart 1: Mission

Display Chart 2: Agreements
Sticky notes (100 per group of six participants)

Preparation:

• Read the lesson and think about how to facilitate it to meet your group's and school's particular needs. Keep in mind that the scripted parts (shown in italics) of the lesson provide only suggested language. Feel free to modify to fit your own style and your group's unique goals.

• On three pieces of poster board or sheets of flip-chart paper, write the following headings (one on each sign):

  • Student to Student
  • Student to Adult
  • Physical Environment

• Hang the three signs on the wall before the meeting.

• Display the 40 Developmental Assets, as well as Display Charts 1 and 2, where all participants can see them.

• Have the sticky notes ready to distribute.

GO

Review of Previous Meetings

1 Welcome participants, thank them for being here, and REMIND them: *We are here today to continue with our efforts to improve our school. What is our mission?*

Refer to Display Chart 1, Mission, and SAY *Our mission is to promote a safer and more supportive school climate, to help build more caring relationships, and to understand the importance of the Developmental Assets.*

ASK *What did we discuss at our last meeting?* (Review.)

Explain that the purpose of ongoing meetings is to remind ourselves of the importance of continuing to make a difference in our school.

Refer to Display Chart 2, Agreements, and give a brief review.

2 SAY *Today we are going to give you an opportunity to brainstorm some ideas to help improve our school.*

3 Arrange participants into groups of six, each group seated in a circle separated from other groups.

4 SAY *We are going to brainstorm ideas in a few moments, but before we begin we need to think about the end result: a more perfect school!*

ASK as a rhetorical question: *What is a more perfect school? a more caring school? a more supportive school?*

5 Lead the participants through a short visualization. In a calm voice, SAY *Close your eyes and imagine a more perfect school. A school that is bright, clean, and inviting. A school where both the adults and the students are kind, caring, and respectful to everyone.*

Pause, and then SAY *Think about how it feels to approach the school from afar. See the outside of the building, look around, see the school grounds and listen to the sounds in the air. Feel how it feels to enter the building. Whom do you see? See the friendly expressions on their faces, hear their kind words as they greet you. Feel how it feels to be warmly welcomed.*

Pass by the office. Whom do you see? What do you hear? Someone calls your name and greets you: "Good morning!" Continue down the hall. Who else greets you? Who are the adults? Who are the students? See their bright eyes and smiles. Walk by the cafeteria. Whom do you see? What do you hear? Hear the laughter and good conversation. Walk over to the doors of the gym and go in. Who is there? What do they say? What do they do? Feel how it feels to be genuinely respected.

Pause, and then SAY *Continue down the hall toward your class. Turn to walk into your classroom. Who sees you? What do they say? What do they do? Feel how it feels to be supported, to be cared for, and to belong.*

Pause, and then SAY *Open your eyes, and come back to the here and now.*

6 ASK *How did that feel to be in a school that seemed so caring?* (Take several responses.)

7 SAY *Let's brainstorm some ideas to make our school the type of school that we just imagined. What do we mean by brainstorming?* **(Generating as many ideas as possible with little thought about the practical implementation of those ideas. We should not judge ideas while we're brainstorming.)**

8 SAY *We're going to consider three general categories for improving the school. They are student to student, student to adult, and physical environment.*

9 Then SAY *Think about your vision for a more perfect school for each of these areas. Then in your small groups, write down or draw a picture of an idea to help promote that vision.*

Pointing to the Student-to-Student display chart attached to a wall, SAY *"Student to student" refers to relationships between students. Some ideas to improve those relationships would be students stopping rumors, students sticking up for other students, and students breaking out of their groups to connect with other students.*

Pointing to the Student to Adult display chart attached to a wall, SAY *"Student to adult" refers* to relationships between students and school adults. School adults may be teachers, coaches, bus drivers, food service workers, counselors, administrators, custodians, and so forth. Some ideas to improve those relationships would be students and teachers eating lunch together, administrators knowing students' names, and students asking teachers for help.

Pointing to the Physical Environment display chart attached to a wall, **SAY** *Finally, physical environment refers to things like student artwork displayed in the hallways, green plants in the lobby, or a friendly and welcoming entrance into the school.*

10 Then **SAY** *Again, think about your vision for a more perfect school for each of these areas. In your small groups, share your ideas to help promote that vision, and then write them on sticky notes. Use as many notes as you wish, but be sure to print neatly and make your ideas as clear and concise as possible. Be sure to generate ideas in each of the three areas.*

EXPLAIN *Then choose someone in your group to be the messenger. The job of the messenger is to collect the written notes. When the messenger has collected about five, he or she walks up to the charts and attaches each of the notes to the appropriate list. When we are done, we will have generated lots of ideas in all three areas. Any questions?*

Give the participants about 15 minutes to complete their task. Ask for a volunteer (adult or student) to help monitor the three charts and to cluster the notes by common themes.

11 When time is up, ask for three student volunteers, one to stand by each chart and to read the notes on that chart.

12 Then **ASK** *What is the purpose of this activity and what does it have to do with our mission of helping to create a more caring and supportive school climate?* (**There is a lot of work to do; there are lots of good ideas; if we apply some of these ideas, we will make a difference.**)

13 **ASK** *What should we do with these ideas?* Reach a consensus that they should be saved, transcribed, prioritized, and that the group should implement the top few ideas.

SAY *In a future meeting we will prioritize items on the lists and plan to implement several of them.*

14 Thank the group for sharing and for making a difference.

Discuss when and where the next meeting will be. If possible, establish the time and place now.

Closure

15 Close with the entire group standing in a circle, and **ASK** *Would anyone like to share anything with this group (feelings, thoughts, words of encouragement, etc.)?*

Thank the group for its commitment and willingness to help make the school a better place. Once again, state the date, time, and location of the next meeting.

WORKING TOWARD A MORE PERFECT SCHOOL

Note: This lesson is a follow-up to Lesson 19.

READY

Summary: This lesson gives participants the opportunity to prioritize the ideas to improve their school that they generated during Lesson 19. Participants also plan to implement at least one idea to help improve their school.

SET

Time Required: 45 minutes

Assets Promoted: Caring School Climate, Community Values Youth, Youth as Resources, Positive Peer Influence, Caring, Planning and Decision Making, Sense of Purpose, Interpersonal Competence

Materials Needed:

List or poster of the 40 Developmental Assets
Poster board or flip-chart paper to make Display Chart 12
Charts listing ideas for a more perfect school from Lesson 19
Flip-chart paper, stand, and markers
Copies of the list of ideas generated during the Lesson 19 brainstorming session

Display Chart 1: Mission
Display Chart 2: Agreements
Display Chart 12: Our Project

Preparation:

- Read the lesson and think about how to facilitate it to meet your group's and school's particular needs. Keep in mind that the scripted parts (shown in italics) of the lesson provide only suggested language. Feel free to modify to fit your own style and your group's unique goals.

- Prior to this meeting, type and print on 8.5" x 11" paper the ideas generated during the Lesson 19 for the three categories (student to student, student to adult, and physical environment).

- Make copies of the list, one for each person.

- Hang on the wall the charts with the lists of ideas created during Lesson 19.

- Make Display Chart 12 (see page 115), using poster board or flip-chart paper.

- Display the 40 Developmental Assets, as well as Display Charts 1 and 2, where all participants can see them.

GO

Review of Previous Meetings

(1) Welcome participants, thank them for being here, and **REMIND** them: *We are here today to continue with our efforts to improve our school. What is our mission?*

Refer to Chart 1, Mission, and **SAY** *Our mission is to promote a safer and more supportive school climate, to help build more caring relationships, and to understand the importance of the Developmental Assets.*

ASK *What did we discuss at our last meeting?* (Review.)

Explain that the purpose of ongoing meetings is to remind ourselves of the importance of continuing to make a difference in our school.

Refer to Display Chart 2, Agreements, and give a brief review.

(2) **SAY** *Today, we are going to give you an opportunity to prioritize the lists of ideas for improving our school that we generated at our last meeting. We will also select at least one of those ideas and plan to implement it.*

(3) Arrange participants into groups of six, each group seated in a circle separated from other groups. Ask that each group select a recorder and a reporter.

(4) **SAY** *Here are three general categories for improving the school that we brainstormed last time we met. They are Student to Student, Student to Adult, and Physical Environment.* Have the large charts that were created at the previous meeting posted on the wall.

Distribute the typed lists with all three categories to all participants. Then assign each group to work on a single category. Depending on the number of groups, some groups may work on the same category.

(5) **SAY** *Our plan is to choose at least one of the listed activities and make it happen in our school. Read over the list and then begin to assign priorities to the items in the list your group has been assigned. When you have the top five items (listed as number 1, 2, 3, 4, and 5), create a plan for making the #1 activity a reality in our school.*

EXPLAIN *The recorder's job is to write down the new list and the group's plan to implement that idea. Your plan could be a simple statement of what you could do to make this happen in the school.*

You need to reach a consensus on ranking the activities. What is a consensus? **(Reaching a general agreement through compromise.)** If students have trouble coming to consensus through discussion, you might suggest that they take a vote.

ASK *Any questions?* Allow about 15 minutes for the groups to work on their assignment.

(6) When the groups are almost finished, be sure each group has a reporter ready to share the group's work.

Then ask for volunteers to report their group's prioritized list and its brief plan. On chart paper, record a basic title for each of the plans they report. Acknowledge each group's work with applause after its report.

(7) **ASK** *Which of these ideas do you think would have the greatest impact on our school? Which of these ideas should we all work on?*

I would like your groups, through consensus, to identify the top two plans—those that you think are practical and have the potential to have a big impact on our school. Recorders, write down your results, your top two ideas, and why you chose those plans. Reporters, be prepared to report your findings.

Allow about 10 minutes for groups to discuss and reach a consensus.

(8) When time is up, ask the reporters to share their findings. Keep a running list of the top two plans selected by the groups.

When all groups have revealed their findings, reach a consensus about which project the large group would like to work on. There are lots of options at this point. If appropriate, you could agree upon and implement more than one plan. Also, if there is good energy in a small group, it is possible for that group to work on its plan. You could also consider implementing one activity from each of the three general categories:

Student to Student, Student to Adult, and Physical Environment.

9 After a plan (or plans) has been determined, refer to Display Chart 12, Our Project, and `SAY` *Now I'd like us all to work together to create the process for which the idea can be implemented by completing the questions on the chart.*

When the chart is completed, discuss any details that are needed to implement the project (such as assignment of tasks, time lines, support, material, etc.). Repeat the process if the group has agreed to implement more than one idea.

10 Then `ASK` *What is the point of this activity and what does it have to do with our mission of helping to create a more caring and supportive school climate?* **(There is a lot to do; there are lots of good ideas; if we apply some of these ideas, we will make a difference.)**

11 Thank the group for sharing and for making a difference.

Discuss when and where the next meeting will be. If possible, establish the time and place now.

Closure

12 Close with the entire group standing in a circle, and `ASK` *Would anyone like to share anything with this group (feelings, thoughts, words of encouragement, etc.)?*

Thank the group for its commitment and willingness to help make the school a better place. Once again, state the date, time, and location of the next meeting.

CLOSURE

LESSON 21: REFLECT, ACKNOWLEDGE, AND CELEBRATE!

REFLECT, ACKNOWLEDGE, AND CELEBRATE!

READY

Summary: The service the participants have given the school community is recognized, reinforced, and acknowledged. Participants create a plan to sustain their service over time. Participants also have an opportunity to reflect on their efforts and to acknowledge one another in a positive way.

SET

Time Required: 2 hours

Assets Promoted: Caring School Climate, Community Values Youth, Youth as Resources, Positive Peer Influence, Caring, Interpersonal Competence, Self-Esteem, Creative Activities, Bonding to School

Materials Needed:

List or poster of the 40 Developmental Assets
Display Chart 1: Mission
Display Chart 2: Agreements
Display Chart 13: In the Long Run . . .
CD player and CD with positive music
Thick- and fine-tip colored markers, at least one of each per participant

Activity Sheet 14: In the Long Run . . .
Certificate of Recognition and Achievement
Large sheets of butcher paper, one per participant
Several rolls of masking tape

Preparation:

- Read the lesson and think about how to facilitate it to meet your group's and school's particular needs. Keep in mind that the scripted parts (shown in italics) of the lesson provide only suggested language. Feel free to modify to fit your own style and your group's unique goals.
- Make copies of Activity Sheet 14 (see page 135), one per participant.
- Make Display Chart 13 (see page 114) using poster board or flip-chart paper and hang it up where all participants can see it.
- Have large sheets of butcher paper (36 inches long) cut and the colored markers readily available.
- Make copies, complete, and ask the principal to sign Certificates of Recognition and Achievement (see page 136), one per participant.
- Display the 40 Developmental Assets, as well as Display Charts 1, 2, and 13 where all participants can see them.

GO

1 Welcome participants and thank them for being here. **EXPLAIN** *This is our last meeting, but it isn't the end of our efforts to improve our school.*

ASK students: *What is our mission?*

Refer to Chart 1, Mission, and **SAY** *Our mission is to promote a safer and more supportive school climate, to help build more caring relationships, and to understand the importance of the Developmental Assets.*

ASK *What did we discuss at our last meeting?* (Review.)

Refer to Chart 2, Agreements, and give a brief review.

2 **SAY** *Since today is our last meeting, we will have an opportunity to reflect on all of our good efforts to improve our school. We have made a difference!*

Distribute the personal folders and allow several minutes for participants to look through the handouts in their folders.

3 Distribute Activity Sheet 14. Refer to Chart 13, and **ASK** *What are you proudest of in your efforts to make a difference in our school? What will you remember to do to continue to make a difference in the long run?*

Allow time for participants to write down their thoughts.

4 Arrange participants into groups of four, each seated comfortably in a circle separated from other groups.

SAY *Please share with your group your thoughts about what you are proud of and what you will remember to do in the future.*

Allow about 10 minutes for discussion.

5 When time is up, **ASK** *Would any of you like to share with the whole group anything you wrote or anything you heard?* (Take several responses, and acknowledge each person with applause.)

Thank the group for sharing and caring. Request that they place the new handout in their personal folder.

6 **EXPLAIN** *In a moment, you will each get a large blank sheet of chart paper. We are going to create an Acknowledgment Poster. When you get your paper I would like you to find a partner and take several markers. Next, I would like you to write your partner's name with thick-tip markers on your paper.*

Allow a few minutes for participants to do this.

SAY *Now I would like you to draw a symbol that your partner strongly identifies with. For instance, your drawing could be a rainbow, mountains, a flag, a music note, or a heart. Your partner will do the same for you. Do this neatly but fairly quickly, since our time is limited.*

ASK *Any questions?* Then **SAY** *When you are done, please hang the Acknowledgment Poster you made for your partner on a wall where everyone can reach it. Don't look at your own Acknowledgment Poster on the wall. You will get it at the close of our meeting.*

Then **SAY** *When all the posters are up, each of us will take a fine-tip colored marker and write on everyone's poster except our own. We will acknowledge each person with words of encouragement, words of support, compliments, and positive thoughts, especially as they relate to our group and our mission of supporting others.*

Please neatly write at least two sentences. (Give an example of an appropriate compliment, such as: Lynn, you are a kind and caring person. I love your enthusiasm, too! Thanks for being my friend.)

ASK *Any questions?* Play some background music that is positive and uplifting. Allow time for participants to complete their task. Circulate around the room to make sure everyone understands the assignment. The adults, including the facilitator, should also have an Acknowledgment Poster.

Allow enough time for everyone to write on all the posters.

7 When time is up, ask everyone to carefully take down their partner's poster, roll it up, tape it, and write their partner's name on the outside of the poster. Collect all the posters in a designated place.

8 When all the posters are collected and everyone is seated, call each person up one at a time, to receive an Acknowledgment Poster and Certificate of Recognition and Achievement. Applaud each person.

Closure

9 Close with the entire group standing in a circle. Share your thoughts and feelings about this group and the work that participants have done.

Then **ASK** *Would anyone like to share anything with this group (feelings, thoughts, words of encouragement, etc.)?*

Thank the group for its commitment and willingness to help make the school a better place.

ADDITIONAL TOOLS

OVERVIEW FOR FACULTY AND STAFF

SAMPLE LETTER TO PARENT/GUARDIAN

SURVEY ADMINISTRATION INSTRUCTIONS

STUDENT SURVEY

OVERVIEW FOR FACULTY AND STAFF

READY

Summary: It is important for all faculty and staff members in your school to be aware of the school climate improvement efforts in which you are engaging. This overview is an introduction for faculty and staff members to the *Safe Places to Learn* group and mission to create a more caring and supportive school climate. You may want to present this during a staff meeting or at any gathering you feel is appropriate.

SET

Time Required: 15 minutes

Materials (all optional):
Handout 1: 40 Developmental Assets for Adolescents
Handout 6: Emily's Story and Sonya's Story (or a story of your own)
Display Chart 1: Mission

Preparation:
- Read Emily's Story or Sonya's story (see pages 101–102) or think of one of your own that addresses similar concerns and/or opportunities
  to make a difference.
- Make copies of Handout 1 (see pages 94–95), one per person.
- Make Display Chart 1 (see page 109) using poster board or flip-chart paper and display it in the front of the room (or simply read the mission from Display Chart 1).

GO

① Welcome staff. Introduce yourself, if necessary.

SAY *We are beginning work with a newly established group of students to help improve the school's climate. First I would like to share a true story to set the stage for this overview.*

Share Emily's Story, Sonya's Story, or a story of your own, possibly highlighting a local incident or experience in which a student (or students) was treated badly and other students had an opportunity to make a difference.

ASK *Do you think there are students who are like Emily (or Sonya) in our school?* (Take several responses.) *Why do students treat others so badly?* (Take several responses.)

② **EXPLAIN** *We are going to intentionally address these and other negative situations that happen in school. We have identified (or will identify) a group of students seen by others as opinion leaders. We will work with these students to empower them to help change the norms that promote and perpetuate meanness and violence at our school. These students will be challenged to act as change agents and to promote the positive norms of respect, common courtesy, tolerance, and kindness. We are also encouraging these students to stand up and not be passive bystanders when mean things happen.*

SAY *We will be meeting periodically with this group, to review each person's efforts to make a difference; to examine their own attitudes, norms, and behaviors; to work on team building; and to develop strategies to engage the whole school in this effort.*

Distribute Handout 1, 40 Developmental Assets for Adolescents.

Refer to Display Chart 1, Mission, and **SAY** *Our mission is to help create a more supportive school climate, to build better relationships among everyone, and to help build Developmental Assets in ourselves and for and with others. Our efforts are grounded in the 40 Developmental Assets, created by researchers at Search Institute.* (Provide information about Search Institute if necessary.) *Some of the assets we will be promoting include Service to Others, Caring School Climate, Positive Peer Influence, Caring, Responsibility, and Personal Power.*

SAY *Even though there are good things going on in our school, there is always room for improvement. We are excited about working with these students to empower them to help improve the climate of the school to help make it a more supportive and safer place to learn.*

Closure

SAY *We are asking for your support in their efforts. Are there any questions?* (Answer any questions.) *If you would like any further information, please feel free to contact me. Thank you for your time!*

Sample Letter to Parent/Guardian

(date)

Dear *(name of parent/guardian),*

Recently, the administration at *(name of school)* completed a process to identify students whose opinions are widely valued and who can lead the way toward shaping a safer, more supportive school environment. Your child was one of those identified as a leader. As a result, we would like your child to participate in an ongoing effort to foster a supportive school climate and improve relationships between and among everyone in the school.

I will be leading students through a series of lessons from a book called *Safe Places to Learn.* We are specifically attempting to change the *norms* (accepted behavior) that promote and perpetuate meanness and violence in the school. These student leaders will be challenged to promote the positive norms of respect, common courtesy, and kindness. The lessons will teach them skills and give them tools they can use in this effort. Among other things, the students will learn about the Developmental Assets that all young people need to be caring, responsible, and happy. This group is made up of student leaders who have the potential to have a powerful impact on the larger student body in reinforcing these positive norms. We plan to have weekly meetings to address these issues.

We want all of our students to feel proud of *(name of school)* and to enjoy being part of our student body. We believe this is crucial to their academic success, as well as their overall well-being. Our vision is to empower students to be a positive force to help create a school climate that is as supportive and safe as possible.

If you have any questions, comments, or concerns, feel free to contact me at *(telephone number).*

Sincerely,

(Sponsor's name)

Please complete, sign, detach, and return the permission slip below.

(date)

I give my permission for (student's name) to participate in (name of school) efforts to help create a more caring school climate.

(Parent/guardian signature)

STUDENT SURVEY ADMINISTRATION INSTRUCTIONS

The initial step, prior to preparing to administer the student survey, is to form a committee of three to five adults. Those adults should know the students well and have insight into the dynamics of their relationships. Committee members could include counselors, a vice principal, teachers, and other adults in the school. It is not generally a good idea to have students on the committee because of confidentiality issues.

Preparing to Administer the Student Survey

1 Determine when to administer the survey. Try to do it near the beginning of the school year at a time when most students are likely to be present—midmorning on a Wednesday, for example.

2 Determine how you'll tabulate the survey—by hand, by machine, or by a combination of both—and make the appropriate arrangements.

3 Determine how many surveys you'll need and make the requisite number of copies.

4 Determine how best to distribute the surveys and to collect them.

5 A week before the survey is to be administered, send a memo to all school adults so they can set aside about 15 minutes to administer the survey.

6 A day before the survey is to be administered, place the appropriate number of surveys and answer sheets in envelopes representing classrooms and other sites throughout the school. Be sure that every student receives a survey.

Administering the Survey

1 Have on hand the requisite number of surveys and pencils.

2 Explain to students the two purposes of the survey: first, to identify people whose opinions are valued and who can lead the way toward shaping a safe and supportive school environment; and second, to get an idea of the state of the school community. Tell students that no one is to sign the survey, so their responses will be anonymous. Say that only a few people will be tabulating the results. Add that the people eventually identified will be asked to join a group that will be asked serve the school community and that the other information will be used to figure out where to focus their efforts.

3 Distribute the surveys.

4 Allow 10 minutes for students to complete the survey.

5 After 10 minutes, collect the surveys, put them in an envelope, and send the envelope to the principal's office.

Tabulating the Survey

What you hope to accomplish:
At the end of this process, you want to end up with a list of students and school adults to invite to participate in the *Safe Places to Learn* group. The people on this list should have the following characteristics:
- Their opinions are valued by others;
- Their opinions are valued by people in a variety of groups outside their primary peer group; and
- They represent the diversity of the school population.

The participants thus are all opinion leaders; the sum of their abilities should be sufficient to influence the entire school community. In selecting these people, you're going to have to make some judgment calls: Does this person, who's mentioned quite a few times but who scores low for influencing other groups, get a higher priority than that person, who isn't mentioned as often but who scores high for influencing other groups? The best way around these puzzles is to envision what you want at the end—a diverse group that is able to effectively promote positive norms in your school community.

You'll also want to get a snapshot of the state of your school community. Responses to the other questions will give you an idea of the extent to which students and school adults perceive the school community as caring, encouraging, respectful, and safe.

What you do after completing the survey:

1 Convene the committee of adults to tabulate the results. Bring everyone together for several hours to complete the process.

2 Review the criteria for identifying the participants.

3 Tabulate the names cited on the surveys. Note how many times each name was mentioned and, for students, their mean score on how much their opinions are valued by students outside their peer group.

4 List all the student subgroups in the school, for example, "athletes," "honors students," "students who hang out at the skateboard park." You may want to make a grid representing these subgroups. The important thing is to be sure that you've selected at least one student from each subgroup.

5 Assign the names of the students cited on the survey to the subgroups.

6 Select students based on the following criteria:
- The frequency with which their names were mentioned;
- Their mean score on the value of their opinions to different students; and
- The degree to which they represent a diversity of groups in the school community.

7 Choose the intended number of students plus one or two alternates in case someone declines to participate.

8 Send a written invitation to join the group to the students who were selected. The following is an example of an invitation:

(date)

Dear *(name of student or school adult)*,
Recently, students and adults at *(name of school)* completed a survey to identify people whose opinions are valued and who can lead the way toward shaping a safe and supportive school environment. You were one of those people. As a result, I'd like to invite you to participate in a group that will, among other things, begin the process of establishing more respectful and supportive relationships between students and adults in our school community.

The first meeting will be held at *(place)* on *(day, date, and time)*.

Students: I would also like to invite your parents or guardians to attend the first meeting. Their attendance or written permission is required for you to participate.

If you can't or do not wish to participate, please let me know by *(day, date)*.

Congratulations on being identified as an opinion leader. I hope to see you soon!

Sincerely,

(name, title)

9 Tabulate the responses to all the other questions and be prepared to present the results to the group and focus on those issues in meetings.

STUDENT SURVEY

Our school would like to identify people whose opinions are valued and who can lead the way toward shaping a safe and supportive school environment. We would also like to get an idea of how people perceive the state of the school community. Please complete this short survey. Think about how you'll respond, and PRINT clearly.

I am ___ male ___ female.

The grade I'm in is ___6 ___7 ___8 ___9 ___10 ___11 ___12.

People Whose Opinions Are Valued

1 Think about the students in your school. Which students' opinions do you value? Which students do you trust to give you accurate information and good advice? Whether or not you know them well, PRINT the names of three of those students in Column 1. Don't worry about the numbers in the other columns; you'll get to circle them in the next questions. For now, just write the names of the students whose opinions you value:

COLUMN 1	COLUMN 2	COLUMN 3
	1 = not at all; 4 = very much	
Names of Students	How Much People in Their Peer Group Value Their Opinions	How Much People Outside Their Peer Group Value Their Opinions
	1 2 3 4	1 2 3 4
	1 2 3 4	1 2 3 4
	1 2 3 4	1 2 3 4

2 Look at the three names you printed above: How much are their opinions valued by people in their own peer group? In Column 2, circle either 1, 2, 3, or 4 for each student. If the student's opinions aren't valued in the group, circle 1 (no value at all) or 2 (low value); if the student's opinions are valued a lot in the group, circle 3 (high value) or 4 (the greatest value).

3 Again, think about these three students: How much are their opinions valued by people outside their own peer group? In Column 3, circle either 1, 2, 3, or 4 for each student. If the student's opinions aren't valued in other groups, circle 1 (no value at all) or 2 (low value); if the student's opinions are valued a lot in other groups, circle 3 (high value) or 4 (the greatest value).

The State of the School Community

For Questions 4–11, circle the number that most closely matches your feeling about the state of the school community in that particular area.

Caring

4 Do you feel that students in your school care about you?

not at all   very much

  1   2   3   4

5 Do you feel that teachers and other adults in your school care about you?

not at all   very much

  1   2   3   4

Encouragement

6 Do you feel that students in your school generally encourage you to do well?

not at all   very much

  1   2   3   4

7 Do you feel that teachers and other adults in your school generally encourage you to do well?

not at all   very much

  1   2   3   4

Respect

8 Do you feel that students in your school generally respect you?

not at all   very much

  1   2   3   4

9 Do you feel that teachers and other adults in your school generally respect you?

not at all   very much

  1   2   3   4

In General

10 Do you feel safe at school?

not at all   very much

  1   2   3   4

11 Do you care about your school?

not at all   very much

  1   2   3   4

12 What is the most important thing that could be done to make your school a better place?

_____

_____

_____

HANDOUTS, DISPLAY CHARTS, AND ACTIVITY SHEETS

40 DEVELOPMENTAL ASSETS FOR ADOLESCENTS

Search Institute has identified the following building blocks of development that help young children ages 12–18 grow up healthy, caring, and responsible.

EXTERNAL ASSETS

Support

1 Family Support—Family life provides high levels of love and support.

2 Positive Family Communication—Young person and her or his parent(s) communicate positively, and young person is willing to seek advice and counsel from parents.

3 Other Adult Relationships—Young person receives support from three or more nonparent adults.

4 Caring Neighborhood—Young person experiences caring neighbors.

5 Caring School Climate—School provides a caring, encouraging environment.

6 Parent Involvement in Schooling—Parent(s) are actively involved in helping young person succeed in school.

Empowerment

7 Community Values Youth—Young person perceives that adults in the community value youth.

8 Youth as Resources—Young people are given useful roles in the community.

9 Service to Others—Young person serves in the community one hour or more per week.

10 Safety—Young person feels safe at home, at school, and in the neighborhood.

Boundaries and Expectations

11 Family Boundaries—Family has clear rules and consequences and monitors the young person's whereabouts.

12 School Boundaries—School provides clear rules and consequences.

13 Neighborhood Boundaries—Neighbors take responsibility for monitoring young people's behavior.

14 Adult Role Models—Parent(s) and other adults model positive, responsible behavior.

15 Positive Peer Influence—Young person's best friends model responsible behavior.

16 High Expectations—Both parent(s) and teachers encourage the young person to do well.

Constructive Use of Time

17 Creative Activities—Young person spends three or more hours per week in lessons or practice in music, theater, or other arts.

18 Youth Programs—Young person spends three or more hours per week in sports, clubs, or organizations at school and/or in the community.

19 Religious Community—Young person spends one or more hours per week in activities in a religious institution.

20 Time at Home—Young person is out with friends "with nothing special to do" two or fewer nights per week.

INTERNAL ASSETS

Commitment to Learning

21 **Achievement Motivation**—Young person is motivated to do well in school.

22 **School Engagement**—Young person is actively engaged in learning.

23 **Homework**—Young person reports doing at least one hour of homework every school day.

24 **Bonding to School**—Young person cares about her or his school.

25 **Reading for Pleasure**—Young person reads for pleasure three or more hours per week.

Positive Values

26 **Caring**—Young person places high value on helping other people.

27 **Equality and Social Justice**—Young person places high value on promoting equality and reducing hunger and poverty.

28 **Integrity**—Young person acts on convictions and stands up for her or his beliefs.

29 **Honesty**—Young person "tells the truth even when it is not easy."

30 **Responsibility**—Young person accepts and takes personal responsibility.

31 **Restraint**—Young person believes it is important not to be sexually active or to use alcohol or other drugs.

Social Competencies

32 **Planning and Decision Making**—Young person knows how to plan ahead and make choices.

33 **Interpersonal Competence**—Young person has empathy, sensitivity, and friendship skills.

34 **Cultural Competence**—Young person has knowledge of and comfort with people of different cultural/racial/ethnic backgrounds.

35 **Resistance Skills**—Young person can resist negative peer pressure and dangerous situations.

36 **Peaceful Conflict Resolution**—Young person seeks to resolve conflict nonviolently.

Positive Identity

37 **Personal Power**—Young person feels he or she has control over "things that happen to me."

38 **Self-Esteem**—Young person reports having a high self-esteem.

39 **Sense of Purpose**—Young person reports that "my life has a purpose."

40 **Positive View of Personal Future**—Young person is optimistic about her or his personal future.

AGREEMENTS

 **Safety**

We agree not to hurt anyone in this group—physically or verbally.

 **Support**

We agree to support others in this group by providing verbal encouragement, listening to others, and sharing ideas.

✓ Respect

We agree to respect others in this group by not interrupting people when they are speaking, keeping things confidential when appropriate, and trying to understand differing points of view.

WORDS
OF ENCOURAGEMENT, OF SUPPORT

I shared my thoughts, feelings, and plans with these people.

CREATING
A CARING, SUPPORTIVE SCHOOL

If ever there were a time to dare to make a difference, to embark on something worth doing, it is now. . .

MY COMMITMENT

_____

_____

_____

_____

BE TRUE
TO YOURSELF!

I'LL BE THE CHANGE

DATE _____

No act of kindness, no matter how small, is ever wasted.

—AESOP

I plan to be courageous, to take a risk, to be an agent of change, to truly make a difference in my school by . . .

_____
_____
_____
_____
_____
_____
_____
_____
_____

This day, these activities, the discussions, and the feelings shared have had an impact on me. Going through this exercise has made me realize . . .

_____
_____
_____
_____
_____
_____
_____

Be the change you wish to see in the world.

—MAHATMA GANDHI

KINDNESS RECOGNITION CARDS

**NO ACT OF KINDNESS,
NO MATTER HOW SMALL, IS EVER WASTED.**
Our group is helping to create a more caring school. We are recognizing those students and staff who are kind and caring. You have received this gift because of a kind act that you offered others. Please wear it as a token of our appreciation and as a gentle reminder for you to continue to show your kindness.
Thank you for what you have done!

**NO ACT OF KINDNESS,
NO MATTER HOW SMALL, IS EVER WASTED.**
Our group is helping to create a more caring school. We are recognizing those students and staff who are kind and caring. You have received this gift because of a kind act that you offered others. Please wear it as a token of our appreciation and as a gentle reminder for you to continue to show your kindness.
Thank you for what you have done!

**NO ACT OF KINDNESS,
NO MATTER HOW SMALL, IS EVER WASTED.**
Our group is helping to create a more caring school. We are recognizing those students and staff who are kind and caring. You have received this gift because of a kind act that you offered others. Please wear it as a token of our appreciation and as a gentle reminder for you to continue to show your kindness.
Thank you for what you have done!

**NO ACT OF KINDNESS,
NO MATTER HOW SMALL, IS EVER WASTED.**
Our group is helping to create a more caring school. We are recognizing those students and staff who are kind and caring. You have received this gift because of a kind act that you offered others. Please wear it as a token of our appreciation and as a gentle reminder for you to continue to show your kindness.
Thank you for what you have done!

**NO ACT OF KINDNESS,
NO MATTER HOW SMALL, IS EVER WASTED.**
Our group is helping to create a more caring school. We are recognizing those students and staff who are kind and caring. You have received this gift because of a kind act that you offered others. Please wear it as a token of our appreciation and as a gentle reminder for you to continue to show your kindness.
Thank you for what you have done!

**NO ACT OF KINDNESS,
NO MATTER HOW SMALL, IS EVER WASTED.**
Our group is helping to create a more caring school. We are recognizing those students and staff who are kind and caring. You have received this gift because of a kind act that you offered others. Please wear it as a token of our appreciation and as a gentle reminder for you to continue to show your kindness.
Thank you for what you have done!

**NO ACT OF KINDNESS,
NO MATTER HOW SMALL, IS EVER WASTED.**
Our group is helping to create a more caring school. We are recognizing those students and staff who are kind and caring. You have received this gift because of a kind act that you offered others. Please wear it as a token of our appreciation and as a gentle reminder for you to continue to show your kindness.
Thank you for what you have done!

**NO ACT OF KINDNESS,
NO MATTER HOW SMALL, IS EVER WASTED.**
Our group is helping to create a more caring school. We are recognizing those students and staff who are kind and caring. You have received this gift because of a kind act that you offered others. Please wear it as a token of our appreciation and as a gentle reminder for you to continue to show your kindness.
Thank you for what you have done!

"BE THE CHANGE" MESSAGE CARDS

**BE THE CHANGE YOU WISH TO SEE
IN THE WORLD!**
Thank you for caring and taking the survey!
Our mission is to help create a more caring school.
Please help us by remembering to act on your plan.
Every day, you have many opportunities to truly make
a difference and to be that positive force in your
world. Please accept our gift as a gentle reminder
for you to . . . **BE THE CHANGE!**

**BE THE CHANGE YOU WISH TO SEE
IN THE WORLD!**
Thank you for caring and taking the survey!
Our mission is to help create a more caring school.
Please help us by remembering to act on your plan.
Every day, you have many opportunities to truly make
a difference and to be that positive force in your
world. Please accept our gift as a gentle reminder
for you to . . . **BE THE CHANGE!**

**BE THE CHANGE YOU WISH TO SEE
IN THE WORLD!**
Thank you for caring and taking the survey!
Our mission is to help create a more caring school.
Please help us by remembering to act on your plan.
Every day, you have many opportunities to truly make
a difference and to be that positive force in your
world. Please accept our gift as a gentle reminder
for you to . . . **BE THE CHANGE!**

**BE THE CHANGE YOU WISH TO SEE
IN THE WORLD!**
Thank you for caring and taking the survey!
Our mission is to help create a more caring school.
Please help us by remembering to act on your plan.
Every day, you have many opportunities to truly make
a difference and to be that positive force in your
world. Please accept our gift as a gentle reminder
for you to . . . **BE THE CHANGE!**

**BE THE CHANGE YOU WISH TO SEE
IN THE WORLD!**
Thank you for caring and taking the survey!
Our mission is to help create a more caring school.
Please help us by remembering to act on your plan.
Every day, you have many opportunities to truly make
a difference and to be that positive force in your
world. Please accept our gift as a gentle reminder
for you to . . . **BE THE CHANGE!**

**BE THE CHANGE YOU WISH TO SEE
IN THE WORLD!**
Thank you for caring and taking the survey!
Our mission is to help create a more caring school.
Please help us by remembering to act on your plan.
Every day, you have many opportunities to truly make
a difference and to be that positive force in your
world. Please accept our gift as a gentle reminder
for you to . . . **BE THE CHANGE!**

**BE THE CHANGE YOU WISH TO SEE
IN THE WORLD!**
Thank you for caring and taking the survey!
Our mission is to help create a more caring school.
Please help us by remembering to act on your plan.
Every day, you have many opportunities to truly make
a difference and to be that positive force in your
world. Please accept our gift as a gentle reminder
for you to . . . **BE THE CHANGE!**

**BE THE CHANGE YOU WISH TO SEE
IN THE WORLD!**
Thank you for caring and taking the survey!
Our mission is to help create a more caring school.
Please help us by remembering to act on your plan.
Every day, you have many opportunities to truly make
a difference and to be that positive force in your
world. Please accept our gift as a gentle reminder
for you to . . . **BE THE CHANGE!**

EMILY'S STORY

Note: The following two stories are true accounts of people who were treated unkindly in school. All names have been changed.

When I was in 7th grade, my family and I moved to a small town in South Carolina. My dad was in the Air Force and we moved often. I lived in eight places from the time of my birth through the time I graduated from high school. Looking back, it was a memorable first day of my 7th-grade year at my new junior high school.

That day, I clearly remember standing at the bus stop near the motel where we were staying. My older brother left earlier on his way to the high school and I was left standing alone waiting for my bus. Moving at the beginning of my 7th-grade year had me worried. I wondered if I would be accepted at my new school. I wondered if I would make new friends and I was really missing my old ones. When the bus arrived, I boarded, turned left past the driver, walked down about six rows, turned, and sat down in an empty seat behind a girl named Emily. I will never forget Emily.

Emily immediately turned around, introduced herself, and asked what my name was. I introduced myself, and then she began to ask me questions like, "Where did you move from?", "Why did you move here?", "Do you know anyone here?" We had a nice conversation that made me feel really welcomed. As I was getting off the bus and walking up to the school with Emily, I was thinking to myself, "This is great. I've barely arrived at school and I already have a friend!" My first impression of Emily was that she was friendly, kind, considerate, and sweet. I remember she had a beautiful smile and, as a 7th-grade boy, I thought to myself, "Emily is cute, too!"

Little did I know that among the students in my new school, Emily had a reputation. She was defined as an outcast, a misfit, one who is to be shunned and teased by all. I don't know

why Emily had such a reputation and may never know why. As a young person, grade school through high school, I always thought of myself as a nice guy. I avoided fights and conflicts, tried to get along and to be nice to all. I don't know why I turned on Emily. I didn't do it maliciously, I didn't go out of my way to hurt her or to be mean to her. I just gradually, over the course of a few weeks, quit talking to her and adopted the norm that Emily was to be excluded. That pattern of my behavior continued through the rest of that school year, after which my family and I moved again to another state.

I don't know what happened to Emily. Looking back on it now, I hope that Emily had it better in high school. I hope and pray today that Emily has a happy life, surrounded with family and friends. For all the pain and rejection she went through, she deserves it.

I look back at the way I acted toward Emily and ask myself, "What was I thinking?" I don't think I *was* thinking! At the time, I did not have the wherewithal to understand all the dynamics of social interactions. I did not understand the concept of negative social norms. I did not understand that it is the good and right thing to stand up against those negative social norms. No one told me that I had power, that I could and should challenge those negative norms. No one told me I could be an agent of change and that I could make a difference. None of my peers nor adults in my life directly guided me, challenged me, or even raised my awareness that it is the right and proper thing to do stand up and to not tolerate unfair treatment of people.

Today, if I could repeat my 7th-grade year, I would do things differently.

SONYA'S STORY

When I was a junior in high school, I lived in a rural area. As the older sister, I drove my 9th-grade brother and myself to town each day in our family car. My brother usually rode the school bus home while I stayed after school to participate in theater practice, but I almost never had to ride the bus. I had ridden the same bus with the same kids for 11 years prior to that, and I had always found it to be a really unfriendly and unsafe place.

One day I had car trouble, so I had to skip theater practice and join my brother on the dreaded bus. There was an unwritten rule that the oldest kids sat in private seats at the rear of the bus, so I found an empty seat back by the other high schoolers. As we loaded passengers from various schools, the bus quickly began to fill up. Eventually even the "big kids" had to move over and share seats.

One of the last people on the bus was another high school girl named Sonya. Sonya was from a really poor family, and her clothes were often visibly soiled. She was very quiet, and she was generally classified as a misfit. She kept to herself whenever possible, but obviously she would need a place to sit on the bus. As Sonya walked down the aisle, even the youngest children started hollering insults at her.

I was amazed at the level of hostility people showed toward her. They made really hurtful comments about her appearance, about her family—everything. Not one person would move over and let her sit down. She gradually made her way to the back of the bus, where most of the kids were even bigger and meaner. When she reached my seat, almost at the very back, I quietly said, "Here. Sit here." She sat down without saying a word.

Unfortunately, people did not stop teasing her once she found a place to sit. One senior boy, Kevin, seemed to make it his mission to terrorize her for the entire 45-minute bus ride. He was sitting behind us, and he said some of the most vulgar, hateful things I've ever heard one person say to

another. Sonya just sat quietly, not even seeming to notice. So I sat quietly, too.

Not getting the reaction he was hoping for, Kevin finally took his behavior to the next level. After insisting several times that Sonya pay attention to him, he spit a gigantic wad of mucus in the back of her hair. Everybody grew quiet. She reached her hand back to feel what had hit her, and she was visibly upset, but she just looked down at her lap and said nothing. Kevin and a few other kids started laughing.

I had finally had enough. I totally lost it. I stood up, turned around, and went on an absolute tirade. I don't remember a lot of the details of what I said, but I know I told Kevin that he was a cruel and horrible person, and everybody else was horrible for laughing and letting him act this way. My whole speech was just a blur of furious tears.

Everyone was quiet for a moment, and then Kevin turned his attention to me. He spent the rest of the ride taunting me, saying that I thought I was better than everyone else, just because I had a car. Nobody joined him, and nobody else laughed at the rest of his jokes. More important, he left Sonya alone the rest of the time.

Initially I was not any better than the other bystanders. Even though I wasn't joining in, I was quietly thinking, "She really does smell funny. And why doesn't she *say* something?" It was only after several minutes that I grew ashamed of myself and finally did something about the situation.

Sonya never spoke a single word to me in my life, before or after that day, but several other kids approached me privately later and thanked me for speaking up. Even though they were scared to say something, they were glad somebody had done it. My brother came home that night and told my parents that I was the bravest person he had ever seen, and he told me later that Kevin never tortured anybody else after that day.

ROLE-PLAY SCENARIO A

Scenario: At the end of the school day, in the hall, you walk toward your locker where two students, both casual friends of yours, are hurtfully teasing another student you don't know.

Your assignment is to develop a strategy that works to help the student being teased.

You will be successful if:
• You resolve the conflict peacefully, and no one gets hurt, physically or emotionally.
• The student being teased is able to walk away.
• The students teasing are able to walk away.
• You remain on reasonably good terms with those doing the teasing.

Create a role play that can meet all the above criteria and present it to the group.

Afterward, answer the following questions:
• What steps did you go through to solve the problem?
• What are the benefits of intervening?
• What are the risks of intervening?
• What is the likelihood that you would actually act to help someone in this situation?

ROLE-PLAY SCENARIO A

Scenario: At the end of the school day, in the hall, you walk toward your locker where two students, both casual friends of yours, are hurtfully teasing another student you don't know.

Your assignment is to develop a strategy that works to help the student being teased.

You will be successful if:
• You resolve the conflict peacefully, and no one gets hurt, physically or emotionally.
• The student being teased is able to walk away.
• The students teasing are able to walk away.
• You remain on reasonably good terms with those doing the teasing.

Create a role play that can meet all the above criteria and present it to the group.

Afterward, answer the following questions:
• What steps did you go through to solve the problem?
• What are the benefits of intervening?
• What are the risks of intervening?
• What is the likelihood that you would actually act to help someone in this situation?

From *Safe Places to Learn: 21 Lessons to Help Students Promote a Caring School Climate.* Copyright © 2007 by Search Institute®; www.search-institute.org. This lesson may be reproduced for educational, noncommercial uses only (with this copyright line).

ROLE-PLAY SCENARIO B

Scenario: Three of your friends begin to talk trash about another friend of yours. They are criticizing that person's clothes and the fact that he is doing well in school. (There may be some jealousy involved.)

Your assignment is to develop a strategy that works to stop the gossiping.

You will be successful if:
- You stop the gossiping peacefully, and no one gets hurt, physically or emotionally.
- Those who are gossiping are less likely to gossip about others in the future.
- You remain on reasonably good terms with those doing the gossiping.

Create a role play that can meet all the above criteria and present it to the group.

Afterward, answer the following questions:
- What steps did you go through to solve the problem?
- What are the benefits of intervening?
- What are the risks of intervening?
- What is the likelihood that you would actually act to help someone in this situation?

ROLE-PLAY SCENARIO B

Scenario: Three of your friends begin to talk trash about another friend of yours. They are criticizing that person's clothes and the fact that he is doing well in school. (There may be some jealousy involved.)

Your assignment is to develop a strategy that works to stop the gossiping.

You will be successful if:
- You stop the gossiping peacefully, and no one gets hurt, physically or emotionally.
- Those who are gossiping are less likely to gossip about others in the future.
- You remain on reasonably good terms with those doing the gossiping.

Create a role play that can meet all the above criteria and present it to the group.

Afterward, answer the following questions:
- What steps did you go through to solve the problem?
- What are the benefits of intervening?
- What are the risks of intervening?
- What is the likelihood that you would actually act to help someone in this situation?

From *Safe Places to Learn: 21 Lessons to Help Students Promote a Caring School Climate.* Copyright © 2007 by Search Institute®; www.search-institute.org. This lesson may be reproduced for educational, noncommercial uses only (with this copyright line).

ROLE-PLAY SCENARIO C

Scenario: In the hallway, before lunch, two of your friends trip or push another student, whom you don't know well. They seem to want to escalate the situation further. You are right in the middle of the situation.

Your assignment is to develop a strategy that works to help the student being threatened.

You will be successful if:
- You resolve the conflict peacefully, and no one gets hurt, physically or emotionally.
- The student being threatened is able to walk away.
- The students who are doing the threatening are able to walk away.
- You remain on reasonably good terms with those doing the threatening.

Create a role play that can meet all the above criteria and present it to the group.

Afterward, answer the following questions:
- What steps did you go through to solve the problem?
- What are the benefits of intervening?
- What are the risks of intervening?
- What is the likelihood that you would actually act to help someone in this situation?

ROLE-PLAY SCENARIO C

Scenario: In the hallway, before lunch, two of your friends trip or push another student, whom you don't know well. They seem to want to escalate the situation further. You are right in the middle of the situation.

Your assignment is to develop a strategy that works to help the student being threatened.

You will be successful if:
- You resolve the conflict peacefully, and no one gets hurt, physically or emotionally.
- The student being threatened is able to walk away.
- The students who are doing the threatening are able to walk away.
- You remain on reasonably good terms with those doing the threatening.

Create a role play that can meet all the above criteria and present it to the group.

Afterward, answer the following questions:
- What steps did you go through to solve the problem?
- What are the benefits of intervening?
- What are the risks of intervening?
- What is the likelihood that you would actually act to help someone in this situation?

From *Safe Places to Learn: 21 Lessons to Help Students Promote a Caring School Climate.* Copyright © 2007 by Search Institute®; www.search-institute.org. This lesson may be reproduced for educational, noncommercial uses only (with this copyright line).

ROLE-PLAY SCENARIO D

Scenario: At the lunch table, three of your friends begin to talk trash about a teacher in your school. They make fun of his appearance, the car he drives, his voice, etc. All three seem to be enjoying it.

Your assignment is to develop a strategy that works to stop the gossiping.

You will be successful if:
- You stop the gossiping peacefully, and no one gets hurt, physically or emotionally.
- Those who are gossiping are less likely to gossip about the teacher or others in the future.
- You remain on reasonably good terms with those doing the gossiping.

Create a role play that can meet all the above criteria and present it to the group.

Afterward, answer the following questions:
- What steps did you go through to solve the problem?
- What are the benefits of intervening?
- What are the risks of intervening?
- What is the likelihood that you would actually act to help someone in this situation?

ROLE-PLAY SCENARIO D

Scenario: At the lunch table, three of your friends begin to talk trash about a teacher in your school. They make fun of his appearance, the car he drives, his voice, etc. All three seem to be enjoying it.

Your assignment is to develop a strategy that works to stop the gossiping.

You will be successful if:
- You stop the gossiping peacefully, and no one gets hurt, physically or emotionally.
- Those who are gossiping are less likely to gossip about the teacher or others in the future.
- You remain on reasonably good terms with those doing the gossiping.

Create a role play that can meet all the above criteria and present it to the group.

Afterward, answer the following questions:
- What steps did you go through to solve the problem?
- What are the benefits of intervening?
- What are the risks of intervening?
- What is the likelihood that you would actually act to help someone in this situation?

From *Safe Places to Learn: 21 Lessons to Help Students Promote a Caring School Climate.* Copyright © 2007 by Search Institute®; www.search-institute.org. This lesson may be reproduced for educational, noncommercial uses only (with this copyright line).

ROLE-PLAY SCENARIO E

Scenario: At the lunch table, three of your friends begin to talk about a fight between two students you don't know. The fight will take place after school. Your friends (and others) seem to be very excited about watching it.

Your assignment is to develop a strategy that works to help stop the fight from occurring.

You will be successful if:
- You help stop the fight, and no one gets hurt, physically or emotionally.
- The people talking about the fight realize that fights between students contribute to a negative school climate and shouldn't be considered entertainment.
- You remain on reasonably good terms with those talking up the fight.

Create a role play that can meet all the above criteria and present it to the group.

Afterward, answer the following questions:
- What steps did you go through to solve the problem?
- What are the benefits of intervening?
- What are the risks of intervening?
- What is the likelihood that you would actually act to help someone in this situation?

ROLE-PLAY SCENARIO E

Scenario: At the lunch table, three of your friends begin to talk about a fight between two students you don't know. The fight will take place after school. Your friends (and others) seem to be very excited about watching it.

Your assignment is to develop a strategy that works to help stop the fight from occurring.

You will be successful if:
- You help stop the fight, and no one gets hurt, physically or emotionally.
- The people talking about the fight realize that fights between students contribute to a negative school climate and shouldn't be considered entertainment.
- You remain on reasonably good terms with those talking up the fight.

Create a role play that can meet all the above criteria and present it to the group.

Afterward, answer the following questions:
- What steps did you go through to solve the problem?
- What are the benefits of intervening?
- What are the risks of intervening?
- What is the likelihood that you would actually act to help someone in this situation?

From *Safe Places to Learn: 21 Lessons to Help Students Promote a Caring School Climate.* Copyright © 2007 by Search Institute®; www.search-institute.org. This lesson may be reproduced for educational, noncommercial uses only (with this copyright line).

ROLE-PLAY SCENARIO F

Scenario: At the lunch table, two of your friends are teasing another student, who usually eats alone. You don't know the victim of the teasing, but you've seen this situation many times.

Your assignment is to develop a strategy that works to stop the teasing.

You will be successful if:
- You stop the teasing peacefully, and no one gets hurt, physically or emotionally.
- Those who are teasing are less likely to tease this student in the future.
- You remain on reasonably good terms with those doing the teasing.

Create a role play that can meet all the above criteria and present it to the group.

Afterward, answer the following questions:
- What steps did you go through to solve the problem?
- What are the benefits of intervening?
- What are the risks of intervening?
- What is the likelihood that you would actually act to help someone in this situation?

ROLE-PLAY SCENARIO F

Scenario: At the lunch table, two of your friends are teasing another student, who usually eats alone. You don't know the victim of the teasing, but you've seen this situation many times.

Your assignment is to develop a strategy that works to stop the teasing.

You will be successful if:
- You stop the teasing peacefully, and no one gets hurt, physically or emotionally.
- Those who are teasing are less likely to tease this student in the future.
- You remain on reasonably good terms with those doing the teasing.

Create a role play that can meet all the above criteria and present it to the group.

Afterward, answer the following questions:
- What steps did you go through to solve the problem?
- What are the benefits of intervening?
- What are the risks of intervening?
- What is the likelihood that you would actually act to help someone in this situation?

From *Safe Places to Learn: 21 Lessons to Help Students Promote a Caring School Climate.* Copyright © 2007 by Search Institute®; www.search-institute.org. This lesson may be reproduced for educational, noncommercial uses only (with this copyright line).

MISSION

To promote a safer and more supportive school climate

To help build more caring relationships among everyone in the school

To understand the importance of the Developmental Assets

* Norms   * Change Agents

AGREEMENTS

 Safety

 Support

 Respect

DISCUSSION QUESTION #1

What are you doing in your school to promote the positive norms of kindness, respect, common courtesy, caring, and support?

No act of kindness, no matter how small, is ever wasted.

—Aesop

Be the change you wish to see in the world.

—Mahatma Gandhi

Never doubt that a small group of committed people can change the world; indeed, it's the only thing that ever has!

—Margaret Mead

DISCUSSION QUESTION #2

What have you done to make a difference in your school?

DISCUSSION QUESTIONS #3 AND #4

What will you remember from our time together and our efforts to make a difference in the school?

What have you done to make a difference in your school?

FIGURE THIS OUT!

Rules

1 The tennis ball must be in motion and clearly pass from person to person in the established pattern. Every person must touch the ball.

2 The tennis ball cannot be suspended, held, or resting anywhere.

3 Timing starts when the tennis ball leaves the first person's hand(s).

4 Timing stops when the tennis ball returns to the first person's hand(s).

TIPS FOR INTERVENING

1 Get involved early.

2 Confront the *behaviors* of the individuals.

3 Safety first.

4 Work one-on-one.

5 Ask adults for help.

6 Don't carry the burden by yourself.

THANK YOU!

- Describe what the person specifically did to have a positive impact on you;

- Thank the person for having done that;

- Encourage the person to do the same for others.

IN THE LONG RUN . . .

What are you proudest of in your efforts to make a difference in our school?

What will you remember to do to continue to make a difference in the long run?

OUR PROJECT

What do we wish to accomplish? (What is the intended result?)

What do we need to implement this idea? (Support, material, time, etc.)

What steps do we need to go through to accomplish the idea? (List the steps.)

What (is the step?) Who (will do it?) When (will it happen?)

1

2

3

4

5

6

How will we know if and when we reached the intended result?
(What will have happened?)

How will we recognize and reward our achievement?

When will we begin?

GUIDELINES FOR CARING (PART 1)

SELF-INVENTORY

Recently we have been challenged to help promote a more caring and supportive school climate. As leaders, we were asked to use our influence to be "agents of change," to be more tolerant and kind, and to look for opportunities to make a difference in other people's lives.

What does this mean? How can I act on these words? How can I use my "power of one"? How can I reach my potential to help, heal, support, challenge, and/or change, for the better, the life of another person? How can I genuinely make a difference? We can't change the world, but we can change our attitude and how we act toward others.

The following are some specific examples of what we can do to truly make a difference, to be that positive force in our school and community. These statements can remind us to "walk our talk" and to be the change, for the better, in our world. You don't have to share your answers with anyone if you don't want to.

Directions: Read the following statements. Answer by circling the number corresponding to the appropriate column. Answer as honestly and accurately as possible.

STATEMENTS	ALWAYS	SOMETIMES	SELDOM	NEVER
Discouraging Negativity				
I gossip or spread rumors that can be hurtful to others.	1	2	3	4
I criticize, tease, or put down others in a hurtful way.	1	2	3	4
I ignore and/or exclude others from my conversations or activities.	1	2	3	4
I physically harm others.	1	2	3	4
Promoting the Positive				
I acknowledge (say hello, smile, etc.) others, including those I don't know.	1	2	3	4
I am considerate toward others.	1	2	3	4
I look for opportunities to be kind toward others.	1	2	3	4
I am open to meeting new people and making new friends.	1	2	3	4
I include others in my conversations or activities.	1	2	3	4

STATEMENTS	ALWAYS	SOMETIMES	SELDOM	NEVER
I encourage others to do well.	1	2	3	4
I listen in class.	1	2	3	4
I do my class work.	1	2	3	4
I do my homework.	1	2	3	4
I follow classroom and school guidelines.	1	2	3	4
I show respect for the adults in school, even though I may have strong disagreements with some of them.	1	2	3	4
Being Courageous, Doing the Right Thing				
I tell people to stop if they begin to tell me rumors that may be hurtful to others.	1	2	3	4
I tell people to stop or distract them if they are being mean and hurtful to others.	1	2	3	4
I ask an adult for help if I am unable or unwilling to help when I see someone being threatened emotionally or physically.	1	2	3	4
I strive to be a positive and healthy role model for my peers and especially for younger children I influence.	1	2	3	4

Study your responses and complete the following statement:

Responding to the Guidelines for Caring self-inventory helped me to learn the following about myself:

_____

_____

_____

GUIDELINES FOR CARING (PART 2)

THE PLAN

The following is my plan to help me be a more positive force for change in my school.

Directions: Review your completed Self-Inventory and then create your plan by explaining your thoughts and intentions for each of the following three categories.

Examine the *Discouraging Negativity* section of your Self-Inventory. What can you do to be less negative in your interactions with others in your school? Be specific.

_____

_____

_____

Examine the *Promoting the Positive* section of your Self-Inventory. What can you do to be a more positive force in your school? Be specific.

_____

_____

_____

Examine the *Being Courageous, Doing the Right Thing* section of your Self-Inventory. What can you do to show more courage and to do the right thing? Be specific.

_____

_____

_____

My intentions are to act on my plan. I have shared it with others in my group. I am asking those in my group to help me, in a positive way, to be accountable for following my plan.

_____   _____

Signature   Date

_____   _____   _____

Witness   Witness   Witness

Be the Change You Wish to See in the World!

ASSET GOAL

I plan to promote asset #_____, _____, in my life.

(name of asset)

I will specifically promote this asset in myself by _____

_____

_____

I will ask for support from our group by requesting that my friend _____ check up on me at times, to be sure I am doing what I said I would do to promote this asset.

_____   _____   _____
Signature   Date   Witness

ASSET GOAL

I plan to promote asset #_____, _____, in my life.

(name of asset)

I will specifically promote this asset in myself by _____

_____

_____

I will ask for support from our group by requesting that my friend _____ check up on me at times, to be sure I am doing what I said I would do to promote this asset.

_____   _____   _____
Signature   Date   Witness

AND MY GOALS ARE . . .

Synonyms for "goal": aim, purpose, hope, wish.

- I have the ability to take responsibility for my health and my life by the decisions I make. By making choices, I use my personal power to shape my own life.
- To help me grow and change, I will set clear and measurable goals in the major areas of my life. I will review my goals often and check on my progress.
- I must remember that I can accomplish almost anything—one step at a time, one day at a time. I promise never to quit trying and, if I need help, I will ask for it.
- When I begin setting my goals, I will work on them for short periods of time. I will then lengthen the time period as I become more successful. For example, I may want to stop drinking soda forever. That's a great goal, but I might start by setting this short-term goal: I will not drink any soda *today*. Then I will lengthen the time as I become more successful.
- I must remember that great distances are covered one step at a time!

Directions: Read the following general categories and the examples. Each category relates directly to an area of Developmental Assets, which is provided in parentheses. Think about that area of your life and of a specific positive goal that would improve that area. Make your goals as meaningful and as relevant to your life as possible.

1 Diet/Nutrition (Positive Values)
Example: I will include more fruits and vegetables in my diet beginning today.

My goal is: _____

_____

2 Exercise (Positive Values)
Example: I will dance, ride my bike, play a sport, or go for a walk for 30 minutes every day this week.

My goal is: _____

_____

3 Education/Career (Commitment to Learning)
Example: I will schedule an appointment with a counselor to discuss my educational/career opportunities within the next two weeks.

My goal is: _____

_____

4 Creative Activities (Constructive Use of Time)
Example: I will seek out and recognize one creative outlet in my life. This outlet may be art, music, dance,

writing, etc. I will pursue this outlet regularly. (I enjoy art, so I will do an art activity on my own or with friends for at least one hour each week.)

My goal is: _____

_____

5 Cultural Competence (Social Competencies)

Example: I will seek out others from different cultures. I will establish a relationship with at least one person with a cultural background that is different from my own. I will learn more about this person and her or his culture.

My goal is: _____

_____

6 Academic Achievement (Commitment to Learning)

Example: I will review my grades and evaluate my academic progress. I will recognize my academic strengths and the subject areas that need improvement. I will determine what I need to do to improve in that area. I may need to study more or I may need some additional help. I will seek out that help if I need it.

My goal is: _____

_____

7 Family Relationships—Parents/Guardians (Boundaries and Expectations)

Example: I recognize that my parent/guardian has my best interests in mind. I will listen when my parent/guardian discusses my boundaries. When I disagree, I will discuss the issue in a calm matter.

My goal is: _____

_____

8 Family Relationships—Siblings (Support/Social Competencies)

Example: I will have patience and not argue with my brother or sister for a whole day/week/month.

My goal is: _____

_____

9 Service to Others—School (Empowerment/Positive Values)

Example: I will intentionally go out of my way every day to say hello to someone who seems isolated or to help someone in school who needs some assistance.

My goal is: _____

_____

⑩ Service to Others—Community (Empowerment/Positive Values)

Example: I will look for opportunities to be helpful in my community. I will visit my elderly neighbor and offer help at least once a week.

My goal is: _____

_____

⑪ Alcohol and Other Drugs—Self (Positive Values)

Example 1: I recognize the harmful consequences that alcohol and other drugs can have on my health, my relationships, and my future. I will seriously examine my attitude about alcohol and other drugs, and I will make a serious effort not to use them anymore. I will not use today! I will surround myself with friends and supporters who encourage me not to use. I will seek out and ask for help if I need it.

Example 2: I am not involved with alcohol and other drugs, and I reaffirm my commitment not to use them. I understand that this choice is not only for my own well-being but also encourages others to make healthy choices.

My goal is: _____

_____

⑫ Alcohol and Other Drugs—Others (Positive Values)

Example: I recognize the harmful consequences that alcohol and other drugs can have on my friend's health, relationships, and future. I will seriously examine my friend's attitude about alcohol and other drugs. I will do all I can do to encourage my friend to make healthy choices. I will not enable her to use by covering for her, lending money to her to buy drugs, making excuses for her, or being used in any way to make it easier for my friend to use. I will express my concern to my friend about her use in a firm but caring way. I will offer my friend help and agree to go with her to seek help if she asks. I will confide in a trusted adult if I need help or am not sure what to do.

My goal is: _____

_____

I plan to pursue all of these goals. I will share these goals with a friend. I am asking my friend to check with me regularly to review my progress.

I, _____, shared my goals with_____.
      (your name)   (partner's name)

Date _____

MY ASSETS/MY GOAL

I am part of a group of students that is learning about Developmental Assets, and we are sharing information about the assets with friends and classmates throughout our school. I would like to do an exercise with you to help you understand the importance of assets in your life. This exercise will take about 30 minutes. All information will remain confidential, and you will be able to keep the document and the list of 40 Developmental Assets when we are done. Thank you!

When we think of the word "assets," we may think of valuable things such as a house, a bank account, or other financial investments. We may also think of personality traits. (For example, his sense of humor is his best asset.) Researchers have identified a list of 40 Developmental Assets. These assets have value, but they can't be measured in terms of dollars and cents. The 40 Developmental Assets can be considered building blocks like relationships, experiences, values, attitudes, and attributes that young people need to be healthy, happy, and successful in their lives. They are called *Developmental Assets* because they help young people develop into healthy, responsible, and caring adults.

PART 1

Please review the list of 40 Developmental Assets. Identify two assets that you consider a strength. Write the asset number and name on the appropriate lines below. Also write down a brief explanation of why this asset is strong in you.

My Strength Assets

1 _____, _____ is my strength asset
    asset #   asset name

because _____

_____

_____

2 _____, _____ is my strength asset
    asset #   asset name

because _____

_____

_____

AGREEMENTS

PART 2

Next, please review the list of 40 Developmental Assets again. This time identify one asset that you would like to call your own, but you don't feel you have now. Write that asset number and name on the appropriate lines below. Also write down a brief explanation of what you can do to begin to build that asset for yourself and what you would like others to help you with. Please be as specific as possible.

My Asset Goal

3 I plan to develop _____, _____, in myself.
        asset #   asset name

I will specifically promote this asset in myself by:

_____

_____

_____

_____

I will ask for support to help me develop this asset by requesting that my friend _____
check on me often, to be sure I am doing what I said I would do to promote this asset in myself and to
support me in the following way:

_____

_____

_____

_____

_____   _____   _____

Signature   Date   Witness

IT PAYS TO BE KIND LOG

Please keep a record of your observations and results!

1 I observed the following event:

Who was kind? _____

What act of kindness was observed? _____

_____

When did it happen? _____

Where did it happen?_____

Results/comments? _____

2 I observed the following event:

Who was kind? _____

What act of kindness was observed? _____

_____

When did it happen? _____

Where did it happen?_____

Results/comments? _____

3 I observed the following event:

Who was kind? _____

What act of kindness was observed? _____

_____

When did it happen? _____

Where did it happen?_____

Results/comments? _____

When you have completed this log, return it to: _____

QUIET CONNECTIONS LOG

Please keep a record of the support you offer!

PART 1

My Name: _____ Date:_____

The person I choose to offer support to, in a quiet manner, is _____.

I think I can support this person in the following ways:

1 _____

_____

2 _____

_____

3 _____

_____

PART 2 (Please review Part 1 every week!)

What Support/When?

The care and support I offered _____ included:

Week 1: _____

_____

Week 2: _____

_____

Week 3: _____

_____

Week 4: _____

_____

Week 5: _____

_____

Week 6: _____

_____

Week 7: _____

_____

Week 8: _____

_____

Week 9: _____

_____

Week 10: _____

_____

Week 11: _____

_____

Week 12: _____

_____

PART 3

The Review

I reviewed this Quiet Connections Log with _____ and would like to say . . .

_____

_____

_____   _____

Reviewer Signature   Date

GUIDELINES FOR CARING: MY PROGRESS

Directions: After reviewing your Guidelines for Caring, Self-Inventory, and Plan, please complete the following two sentences:

I am doing well promoting the positive norms by _____

_____

_____

I want to improve by _____

_____

_____

GUIDELINES FOR CARING: MY PROGRESS

Directions: After reviewing your Guidelines for Caring, Self-Inventory, and Plan, please complete the following two sentences:

I am doing well promoting the positive norms by _____

_____

_____

I want to improve by _____

_____

_____

GUIDELINES FOR GIVING THE *CHANGING THE NORMS* SURVEY

Please take this task seriously and remember to operate under the rule of confidentiality!

1 Obtain a clean copy of both parts of the survey.

2 Decide to whom you plan to give the survey.

3 Ask that person whether he or she is willing to take the survey (remember to explain and stick to the rule of confidentiality).

4 Arrange a quiet place and time to share the survey (allow at least 15 minutes).

5 Be seated at a table and set a serious tone when you are introducing the survey.

6 Read the directions clearly to the person.

7 Read each question clearly and allow time for the person to respond. Circle the appropriate corresponding number.

8 Put down your pencil when the last number on the survey is circled. Review with your friend the responses. Ask, "What did you learn or realize from doing this survey?" Help your friend clarify her or his thoughts and then write them down in the space provided at the bottom of the survey.

9 Turn to the next page, Changing the Norms (Part 2): My Plan. Read the directions on the top of the page.

10 Review with your friend her or his responses to *Discouraging Negativity*. Help your friend clarify what he or she is willing to do to discourage the negative norms. Allow your friend to write her or his thoughts down on the plan.

11 Review with your friend her or his responses to *Promoting the Positive*. Help your friend clarify what he or she is willing to do to encourage the positive norms. Allow your friend to write her or his thoughts down on the plan.

12 Review with your friend her or his responses to *Being Courageous, Doing the Right Thing*. Help your friend clarify what he or she is willing to do to encourage the positive norms. Allow your friend to write her or his thoughts down on the plan.

13 Ask your friend to review the final plan with you. Ask her or him whether it is possible to act on this plan and whether he or she is willing to try. Then ask your friend to sign and date it on the appropriate lines. You sign as a witness. Explain that you are there to support your friend's plan and that you will check in from time to time.

14 Thank your friend for her or his time and commitment. Offer the gift (wristband or other gift) and/or the "Be the Change" Message Card as an inspirational reminder to "be the change" and to act on her or his plan. Give the survey and plan to your friend and ask that he or she review it from time to time.

15 Report your friend's name and her or his general response to the group's adult sponsor, and obtain another survey. Also, get another gift and/or message card from your sponsor. Repeat the process with a different friend.

CHANGING THE NORMS (PART 1): SURVEY

A group of students in our school is working to promote a more caring and supportive school climate. We are trying to be more tolerant, kind, and caring, and to look for opportunities to make a positive difference for others in our school. We are asking you to join us in this movement to promote a more caring school.

What does this mean? How can we act on the words? How can we use our individual "power of one"—the potential for each of us to help, to heal, to support, to challenge, and to change, for the better, the life of another person? How can we genuinely make a difference? We can't change the world, but we can change our attitude and how we act toward others.

The following are some specific examples of what we can do to truly make a difference, to be that positive force in our school and community. These statements can serve as a reminder for us to "walk our talk" and to be the change, for the better, in our world.

Directions: I will read several statements. After each statement, you tell me with what frequency the statement is true for you. Your choices are Almost Always, Sometimes, Seldom, or Never. I will circle the number corresponding to the appropriate answer. Please answer as honestly and as accurately as possible. Your answers are completely confidential and, when we are done with the survey, it is yours to keep.

STATEMENTS	ALMOST ALWAYS	SOMETIMES	SELDOM	NEVER
Discouraging Negativity				
I gossip or spread rumors that can be hurtful to others.	1	2	3	4
I put down or tease others in a hurtful way.	1	2	3	4
I ignore and/or exclude others from my conversations or activities.	1	2	3	4
I physically harm others.	1	2	3	4
Promoting the Positive				
I acknowledge (say hello, smile, etc.) others, including those I don't know.	1	2	3	4
I am considerate toward others.	1	2	3	4
I look for opportunities to be kind toward others.	1	2	3	4
I am open to meeting new people and making new friends.	1	2	3	4
I include others in my conversations or activities.	1	2	3	4

STATEMENTS	ALMOST ALWAYS	SOMETIMES	SELDOM	NEVER
I encourage others to do well.	1	2	3	4
I listen in class.	1	2	3	4
I do my class work.	1	2	3	4
I do my homework.	1	2	3	4
I follow classroom and school guidelines.	1	2	3	4
I show respect for the adults in school, even though I may have strong disagreements with some of them.	1	2	3	4
Being Courageous, Doing the Right Thing				
I tell people to stop if they begin to tell me a rumor that may be hurtful to others.	1	2	3	4
I tell people to stop or distract them if they are being mean and hurtful to others.	1	2	3	4
I ask an adult for help if I am unable or unwilling to help if someone is being threatened emotionally or physically.	1	2	3	4
I strive to be a positive and healthy role model for my peers and especially for younger children I influence.	1	2	3	4

Study your responses from the above and complete the following statement.

Responding to the Changing the Norms Survey helped me to learn the following about myself:

_____

_____

_____

_____

CHANGING THE NORMS (PART 2): MY PLAN

The following is my plan to help me be a more positive force for change in my school.

Directions: Review your completed Changing the Norms Survey.

Create your plan by explaining your thoughts and intentions for each of the following categories.

Examine the *Discouraging Negativity* section on the survey. What can you do to be less negative in the ways you interact with others in your school? Be specific.

_____

_____

_____

Examine the *Promoting the Positive* section on the survey. What can you do to be a more positive force in your school? Be specific.

_____

_____

_____

Examine the *Being Courageous, Doing the Right Thing* section on the survey. What can you do to show more courage and to do the right thing? Be specific.

_____

_____

_____

My intentions are to act on my plan. I shared my plan with my friend. I am asking my friend to help me, in a positive way, to be accountable for following my plan.

_____   _____   _____
Signature   Date   Witness

Be the Change You Wish to See in the World!

UNDER MY WING

I plan to intentionally make a positive difference for _____

(person's name)

I plan to make a difference by doing the following: _____

_____

_____

I will ask for support from our group by requesting that my friend _____ check on me often, to be sure I am doing what I said I would do to make a difference.

_____   _____
Signature of Witness   Date

UNDER MY WING

I plan to intentionally make a positive difference for _____

(person's name)

I plan to make a difference by doing the following: _____

_____

_____

I will ask for support from our group by requesting that my friend _____ check on me often, to be sure I am doing what I said I would do to make a difference.

_____   _____
Signature of Witness   Date

INVITATION

A group of students in our school is working to create a more caring school. To further this goal, we are inviting other students to join us for ___ minutes to play games and to get to know each other better. We are inviting you to share in the fun! Our only requests are that you arrive on time with a positive attitude and be ready to participate fully in the activities.

When: _____

Where: _____

Bring: Great attitude and playful spirit!

Thank you!
We look forward to seeing you!

INVITATION

A group of students in our school is working to create a more caring school. To further this goal, we are inviting other students to join us for ___ minutes to play games and to get to know each other better. We are inviting you to share in the fun! Our only requests are that you arrive on time with a positive attitude and be ready to participate fully in the activities.

When: _____

Where: _____

Bring: Great attitude and playful spirit!

Thank you!
We look forward to seeing you!

IN THE LONG RUN . . .

What are you proudest of in your efforts to make a difference in our school?

_____

_____

_____

_____

_____

_____

_____

What will you remember to do to continue to make a difference in the long run?

_____

_____

_____

_____

_____

_____

_____

Certificate of Recognition and Achievement

for service to the school community

NAME

DATE

NAME OF SCHOOL

SPONSOR

PRINCIPAL

ACKNOWLEDGMENTS

The paths we take and the destinations we attain on this journey through life can be intriguing. This publication's roots began with a phone call in the spring of 2002. On the line that day was Clay Roberts, my friend, colleague, and mentor. He invited me to be part of a group of trainers to implement the Kansas Health Foundation's efforts to spread the asset message, particularly to help improve the climate in high schools throughout that state. Clay was heading up that team of exceptional people from Kansas and around the nation. The team included Marilyn Peplau, Chris Beyer, Elliot Herman, Miffy Ruggiero, and Emily Roberts. The initial design and writing of this project, dubbed *Take a Second, Make a Difference Goes to School*, were undertaken by the creative and prolific writer Neal Starkman. Our hosts from the Kansas Health Foundation included Jeff Usher, Vera Bothner, and Steve Williams. Having the opportunity to collaborate and co-train with such a talented and passionate group of people was a trainer's dream. I greatly appreciate the hard work and effort of all these people, which provides the foundation for this book.

In 2003 Marilyn Peplau and I had the opportunity to transform *Take a Second, Make a Difference* into a one-day retreat called *Change of Heart*, which is now offered nationwide by Search Institute. The impetus for the creation of this publication was to address the need for ongoing training after the *Change of Heart* retreat. I later broadened its scope and believe this book provides an excellent platform for launching any effort led by youth to help create a caring, supportive climate at any school—whether or not it has gone through the *Change of Heart* training.

I'm thankful to several people from Search Institute who contributed to and supported me in this effort, including Claudia Hoffacker, my thoughtful, competent, creative, and efficient editor; Lynette Ward, who is always open to new ideas; Lisa Sheff, for her positive attitude and hard work; Tenessa Gemelke, for sharing her powerful story; and Peter Benson, who is an inspiration and gave his blessing for Search Institute to publish this book.

Others who have supported, contributed, or encouraged the effort to create *Safe Places to Learn* include Charlie Bell, Esther Carbajal, Mimi Petritz-Appel, Laurie Bassett, Kevin Soule, Amy Rush, Terry Jaurequi, Casey Molloy, Tim Duffey, Donna Duffey, Pat Fecteau, Rod Dugan, Sue Allen, Don MacIntyre, Keith Pattinson, Julie Vincek, Anita Davis-DeFoe, Jessica Broz, Ilyana Marks, Pam Parrish, Randy Thomas, Scott Butler, Betsy Gabler, Stephanie Drakulich, Susan Wootten, and Nathan Eklund.

The great influence of my former training partner and friend forever from Alaska, Stan Mayra, is reflected in this book. Earnie Broughton, my almost-lifelong friend and brother from a different mother, has been a positive force and a great measure of encouragement for the writing of this book. Lynn, my wife of 25 years, and my daughters, Amanda and Kimmi, have been my tireless supporters and encouragers, for which I am most grateful.

Finally, I would like to thank all the students and staff from New Hampshire to California, Minnesota to Texas, Alaska, and British Columbia, whom I have had the honor and privilege to work with over the years. They have helped shape my journey, as well as the outcome of this book.

PAUL SULLEY

About the Author

Paul Sulley has worked in the field of positive youth development for more than 20 years. He has presented various training events to tens of thousands of adults and young people throughout North America. Sulley has been a Search Institute trainer since 2003 and has presented dozens of *Change of Heart* training retreats throughout the nation. He and his wife, Lynn, have two teenage daughters, Amanda and Kimberly, and live just outside of Spokane, Washington.